Relationships
for
LIFE

How to Improve Yourself and the
Relationships around You

Richard Marks, PhD with Johnny Earl Jones

authorHOUSE®

AuthorHouse™
1663 Liberty Drive
Bloomington, IN 47403
www.authorhouse.com
Phone: 1-800-839-8640

First published by AuthorHouse 2/28/2011

ISBN: 978-1-4520-8206-6 (sc)
ISBN: 978-1-4520-8207-3 (hc)
ISBN: 978-1-4520-8205-9 (e)

Library of Congress Control Number: 2010914958

Printed in the United States of America

This book is printed on acid-free paper.

Interior art photos copyright by Bodway Photography
Photographer: Dixie Harrington

Some scripture quotations contained herein are taken from the Holy Bible, King James Version and New Living Translation.

To my precious friend and wife, Louella, for all the years of loving me, being by me, and believing in me. And to Trey, Madison, and Jesse, the most wonderful children a man could ask for: I am a better man because of you all.

About the Author

Dr. Richard Marks earned a PhD in Psychology and Counseling, a Master of Arts in Marriage and Family Therapy and an M.A. in Religious Education from Southwestern Baptist Theological Seminary. In addition to being a Licensed Professional Counselor, he is also an ordained minister. Rick serves as the Executive Director of Marriage for Life, Inc., and is the author of the Enriched Relationship series of relationship materials. Rick also served as a Commissioner on the Florida Commission of Marriage and Family Initiatives from 2003-2007 and conducts retreats and seminars for  youth, singles, engaged couples as well as marriage retreats and family life seminars and retreats for wounded soldiers with the US Army. Dr. Marks has been a keynote speaker in conferences such as Smartmarriages, AACC, North American Conference for Divorced and Separated Catholics, and Association of Marriage and Family Ministries. He writes articles for local publications and has been on national radio and television shows such as the 700 club. Rick appears on WJXT's The Morning Show in Jacksonville for the Making Marriage Work segment.

Rick and Louella have journeyed together in marriage since 1984 and have three children, Trey, Madison, and Jesse. They can be contacted through their website at www.marriageforlife.org.

About the Author

Johnny Earl Jones is a writer who believes that "life is an adventure and God is in control." Unashamed of his faith in Christ, he believes that every step of the way we should encourage others and point them to their only hope: Jesus the Savior.

Johnny has a Bachelor of Arts degree in Literature from the University of North Florida, with a minor in Journalism. He is author of the Christian Fantasy Adventure Romance novel called *Lifespring* and the encouragement book *You're Gonna Make It: Extreme Encouragement during Discouraging Times.* He has appeared on local radio program **Journeys with Christ** for several radio interviews. He is also a motivational and encouragement speaker, teaches Single Adult Bible Study, and sings in the Sanctuary Choir at North Jacksonville Baptist Church, which is aired nationwide on the Sky Angel Network.

His wife is Jobi, wonderful and wise, and Chezney is his energetic teenage daughter.

Contents

* 1 *

THE ANATOMY OF A RELATIONSHIP

We all have them. We can't live without them. Because of them, life can be difficult and even painful. Without them existence would be dull. I'm talking about relationships, and individuals have myriads of them to wade through. Our lives span a wide spectrum of relationships: parents, children, spouses, friends, co-workers, bosses, employees, church-folk, acquaintances, strangers, mentors, protégés, teachers, students, God, and other interests.

Obviously, each relationship is unique and has different dynamics. You wouldn't communicate the same way to your spouse as you would to fellow co-workers. And your affinity with God should be distinctive compared to your conversation with a stranger. Because we travel through such a wide range of relationships, we have to learn the different dialects of each one to enjoy them fully. This book provides the useful tools needed to enhance yourself and your daily relationships to be healthy, vibrant, and connected.

We interact with a variety people who play different roles in our lives, but here's the problem: many of our relationships are unhealthy. We don't often practice the deftness necessary in building strong, lasting, loyal, and trusting interaction. The main reason we don't develop our relationships to their optimum is because we don't know how and because we already have ingrained in us examples set by our parents, friends, or some authority figure. We don't have to continue destructive or damaging habits though.

When we educate ourselves on how to gain, protect, and enhance our relationships, frustration dwindles while understanding and compassion begin to bloom.

Each relationship role has exclusive rules to be adhered. But to succeed in those there are basic tenets that can be followed and practiced.

Who wants a lifetime of shallow, meaningless relationships?

Who wants to be so consumed with success and wealth that you neglect all who are dearest to you? When a person is terribly ill or despondent, they never ask for the company of their sports car or a pile of their cash piled around the table lamp. In times of need, you would like to know there are people by your side who care about you and love you. No material good can comfort you; therefore, none should supersede your daily closeness with people.

That is the issue: closeness. We deal with people everyday. We live with spouses and children, or with parents, relatives or guardians. We make important decisions that affect the very lives of other individuals. But is there any semblance of closeness, of trust, or of emotional vulnerability? Sadly, for the majority of people the answer is No.

Marriages get strained and torn apart.

Friendships grow cold and fade into nothing.

Employers and employees draw lines in the sand and declare each other enemies.

Why are relationships so easy to start but so difficult to sustain?

There is a euphoria attached to meeting someone new, portraying an image to that person, and causing that individual to think you are something special. But when the novelty wears off, the mask is removed, and reality sets in, the relationship takes on the need for maintenance and communication. Since many don't know how to do this, they don't endure or bring reconciliation when misunderstanding or conflict results. You may drop that relationship like a soft drink bottle that's been sucked dry and move on to the next one, carrying those same patterns into each new relationship.

In my young adult years I (Johnny) never had any meaningful friendships, nor was I close to my parents or siblings. I was what you'd call a "navy brat," which meant I was the son of a sailor whose family would be uprooted and moved every six to eighteen months. I didn't learn relational skills from my folks because either my dad was out at sea for extended periods, or if when he was home, he and my mom were always in conflict, particularly since both drank heavily. Since we were always on the move, I learned how to make friends quickly because I knew I'd lose them quickly. Never was there a time when I practiced longevity skills in friendships, because if someone disappointed me and hurt me, I'd hold a grudge and not extend forgiveness. That relationship would die, but so what? I'd be moving in a couple of months again anyway and make new acquaintances. That pattern lasted even into my adult years, but when my own Navy tour was over and I decided to settle down, I discovered the harsh truth that lack of relationship skills was not conducive to meaningful, lasting interaction. I realized if I held grudges and was unforgiving to everyone who I perceived had wronged me, it wouldn't be long before I was isolated and alone.

Many of us have gotten to the point where we feel isolated and alone.

You might think, "The reason why I'm not appreciated is because nobody understands me. If people weren't so shallow they'd take the time to know me then they'd like me. They don't know what they're missing out on."

The main problem with building relationships is we place the bulk of the responsibility on the other person while shouldering little or none of it. Each must give and take to make it succeed. Readiness to change, enhance, and pardon must be instilled in you if you want to interact maturely. As Dr. James McDonald, pastor of Harvest Bible Church says, "Each relationship must have several big forgivenesses and a truckload of small forgivenesses."

We are going to look at skills in this book that will dramatically improve all your relationships because what is going to be challenged is the way you think about yourself, the reason you act and react a certain way, as well as why other people will either accept or reject your actions, words, and attitudes.

The anatomy of a relationship seems complex, but when you choose to put effort into it and are willing to sacrifice your pride and selfishness, your interaction with others becomes your greatest joy and treasure.

You will discover "Aha" moments as you turn the pages, when you realize why certain things you said or did produced negative results. You'll also see how relationships can be knit so tightly through communication tools that you'll never want to go back to living in an environment of misunderstanding. You'll gain such confidence you'd be embarrassed to throw a "pity party."

There are several components that make a relational anatomy:

--Emotions

--Communication

--Understanding

--Closeness

--Rationality

--Perception

--Sacrifice

--Purpose, et al.

Unashamed, this guide to the foundation of relationships is Biblically based. We'll turn to the Creator of relationships and His wisdom. Who better to tell us how to interact effectively than the One who made us?

Relationships aren't just about having people in our lives; it's about living a life allowing you the privilege of being a blessing, a joy, an encouragement, and an example to others. Relationships are more than just taking what someone else has to offer, but giving back to the relationship so it can grow and flourish.

Jesus Christ was once asked, "Which is the most important commandment?"

He replied, "You must love the Lord your God with all your heart, all your soul, and all your mind. This is the first and greatest commandment. A second is equally important: love your neighbor as yourself."

The Lord emphasizes it's all about relationships, with God and with your fellow man.

The Us-ness Principle

Every relationship has its specific needs for maintenance and prosperity. Each one can operate efficiently when you have all the aspects in place. Some have inferred it takes three people to make a great relationship; this definitely is true in the case of the most intricate human relationship—marriage. The principles we're about to look at will work in all relationship circles and improve them vastly.

Let's take a marriage as an example. The first and most important person in that marriage is Almighty Christ Jesus, the Creator and Sustainer of all things. Christians know Christ is their source of strength, wisdom, peace, knowledge, joy, and love. As long as Christ is the foundation of anything you do, the favor and goodness of God rests on all your endeavors. Christ is the one who makes marriages work. He guides us. He protects us from the evil one's spiritual attacks when we're following Christ. He's given us spiritual principles and promises to bless our every day lives. Needless to say, Christ is paramount in the upkeep of a great marriage. Obviously, the other two people are the man and the woman, but let's say Jesus steps back for this illustration. We still need three people to make a successful marriage. It takes him, her, and—'Us.'

"'Us' is the third person?" you may ask.

Yes. The Bible describes briefly the world's first marriage ordained by God Himself. Listen to what Adam said.

"At last!" Adam exclaimed. "She is part of my own flesh and bone! She will be called 'woman' because she was taken out of man." This explains why a man leaves his father and mother and is joined to his wife, and the two are united into one (Genesis 2:23-24).

Before matrimony, there were two separate and distinct personalities who are interested in each other. Each has their own history, experiences, likes, and dislikes. When they marry something happens: the two become one. So where does 'Us' come in? And why is it so important? 'Us' is two individuals dying to their own agendas and lovingly sacrificing for the good of the other.

You might say, "If both of us are doing nothing but trying to make the other person happy, then neither us of will really be fulfilled."

When two become 'us' it doesn't mean they stop being individuals with their own needs, but it does mean when your mate wants to be with you and do things you don't particularly care for, you are willing to accept it and enjoy your time together.

My wife likes to visit the mall. I detest going there. But if she wants to go and she wants me by her side, even though I don't care for it, 'Us' likes it. 'Us' is the unity that is built between two people that leads to intimacy.

Intimacy isn't necessarily sexual; that's only reserved for marriage because wedlock was designed for the safety of the couple. True intimacy means you've developed a closeness that cultivates trust and peace. Sometimes intimacy can grow so deep your mate doesn't even have to say anything to you, and you'll know what they need. Us-ness exterminates selfishness and breeds intense love and friendship. Marriage is not a 50/50 proposition. Neither is any other relationship. If one person gives 50%, and the other gives 50%, they are doomed. If both aren't giving 100% each to the marriage, or to any other relationship, it'll be strained by selfishness and self-centeredness.

If the King of the Universe places top priority on relationships with Himself and with others, we should receive that wisdom and realize the greatest treasures in this life have nothing to do with what we own or how big our bank account is, but who we know and enjoy being with.

The evangelist Billy Graham was once invited as a guest to a tropical island where he had lunch with an extremely rich businessman. This businessman lived in a marvelous mansion by the sea. He had a huge pool, a scenic view, a personal dock where moored was a private boat. The man seemed to have everything, but he confessed to Dr. Graham that his life seemed so empty. His life consisted of the things he was able to achieve, but it was void of any meaningful relationships. Later Dr. Graham visited the other side of the island where an elderly pastor lived. This pastor had a simple home, and he lived in poverty. His wife was sick, so he spent much of his day caring for her. Billy Graham spent the afternoon with him and couldn't help but notice the stark contrast between this aged pastor and the wealthy businessman. The businessman owned immense wealth, but still felt hollow because he lacked the riches every person needs: a loving relationship with the Lord Jesus Christ and with friends and loved ones. Although owning little, the pastor was full of life and excitement. He was rich in his relationships with the Lord, his wife, his friends, and his congregation.

* 2 *

IMAGE IS EVERYTHING

BUILDING THE REAL 'YOU'

When I was a graduate professor in Virginia Beach, I was approached by one of my female master's students and she inquired, "Dr. Marks, can I ask you a personal question?"

"Of course," I replied.

"Why are you so obnoxious?"

Fair question, I thought before I replied, "It's my ministry."

"What?"

"It's a ministry I have."

"What do you mean by that?" she asked, bewildered.

I answered her question with my own. "What's the number one mental health problem in America?"

After a moment of thought, she begins listing several DSM4 diagnoses like schizophrenia and bipolar disorder.

"No, think about it. What do most Americans struggle with outside of DSM4s?"

"Well, self-image, I guess."

"Exactly. Americans are plagued by low self-esteem," I said before I looked to her quizzically and asked, "Why do people have low self-esteem?"

"Because they have tendency to compare themselves to people they think are better or are more prosperous than they are," she said.

"Exactly. Now here's how it works—when people see me acting the way I do, they inherently think to themselves, at least I'm not like him. At that moment their self-esteem raises. It's a ministry of mine."

"That's bizarre," she said and walked away.

Everyone longs for healthy self-esteem. We all want to portray a positive, confident self-image. So why does it seem to evade so many? Maybe it's because we don't know what a healthy self-image is supposed to look like.

What is self-esteem?

Some might say self-esteem is simply knowing who you are. Others might say its liking who you are. Yet others might say it's confidence you have in yourself, or it's how you perceive yourself. These all sound good but they aren't the foundation of self-esteem. Can you perceive yourself a certain way and have a good self-esteem? Sure. Some serial killers have great self-esteem. They are good at their trade, and they have confidence in themselves.

So what really is self-esteem?

Simply, it's the value and worth you place on yourself.

Well, if self-esteem is the value and worth you place on yourself, and most people have a poor self-esteem, it would seem only obvious not many people look favorably on themselves. Until you can view yourself as having intrinsic dignity and merit, it will be hard for you to establish lasting, healthy relationships with other people. Before you begin tackling the intricacies of interacting with other folks, you must nail down exactly who you are and what you stand for. By knowing who you are and valuing yourself as the person God made you to be, you portray the confidence and self-esteem so many long for. You will become winsome and a joy to others. And you won't suck the life out of people.

If you've got a poor self-image how do you refashion it? Can you totally undo what a lifetime of wrong thinking has formed you into?

The answer is a simple 'yes.' The pathway is quite intricate and will take effort. Change won't happen aside from self-sacrifice, self-evaluation, and hard work. As the saying goes, "If you want to be someone else, change your mind." You don't have to live your life as a victim, a toadie, or an aimless follower. You can take charge of your life by changing your mind, your attitude, and your level of faith. We are about to walk a path which can transform you forever. Keep your mind alert and be prepared to be challenged.

Where do people develop their self-image? Some may say from the family. What about family helps you develop worth? Maybe, it's when parents give you feedback that the things you accomplish gives you value. "You know, I'm really proud of you when you get good grades." Would that build your self-esteem? One of the things we have today, even in Christian homes, is a performance-based identity and value. According to that, all of your value and worth is based on how well you perform or achieve the goal someone else has for you.

Many of us carry the duel persona of a false self and a real self. The real self is who you actually are on the inside—the sometimes scared, sometimes doubtful, and the sometimes unworthy-feeling individual. Today, most in America who don't like some part of themselves, dragging around a low self-image, will choose to live in a false self which is only a façade, a fake. Why do people do that?

Dr. Mike Murdock said, "Everyone's in search of a feeling."

If pretending to be something you're not makes you feel better about yourself, then that's how you'll live. There's a great danger with that. When you live in the false self you become vulnerable and easy to manipulate. A discerning mind can easily discover a person living in their false self, and a crafty individual knows the exact words to say, and how and when to say them to sway their emotions, thus controlling them. The right words can make you feel loved, and that will make you feel more confident. Some people can give you certain words to generate a certain feeling, and you'll think, *Wow! I'm loved and accepted here.* But what you don't realize is you're being used, manipulated, and controlled for another's benefit. A person who relies on some else's words to make them feel good is immature—emotionally and relationally. The person with the smooth words will continue to control, and that sorry scenario is produced by a low self-image. You will do things that you'd not necessarily do if you had a positive self-image. Self-respecting people have a healthy self-image.

Does the Bible support the idea we should have a healthy self-esteem?

Candidly, I declare the Bible isn't a psychology book. Now there are some Christians who think the Bible is a psychology book, but I disagree with them.

I had a lady who came and challenged me. She didn't like me—she actually didn't know anything about me—but she judged me because I had a psychology degree. She bantered with me, trying to prove that psychology was evil. I wouldn't engage in that kind of argument because no one wins. But I'll never forget that she had her Bible and she patted it, saying, "This is the only psychology book I ever need."

"Ma'am," I said, "Please don't ever lower God's Word to the level of a psychology book. It isn't. There may be psychologically related principles in there that we can glean from it to affect our humanity, but it isn't a psychology book."

The words self-esteem and self-image are not in the Bible, but there are scriptures that would suggest we need to have this thing we call self-esteem.

…I am fearfully and wonderfully made… (Psalm 139:14)

…[The Lord] will rejoice over you with great gladness. With His love, He will calm all your fears. He will exult over you by singing a happy song (Zephaniah 3:17).

Despite all our troubles, we are more than conquerors through Christ who loved us (Romans 8:37).

…Nothing in all creation will ever be able to separate us from the love of God that is revealed in Christ Jesus our Lord (Romans 8:38).

If the King of the Universe places value on me as a person that should affect the way I see myself.

The Self-Esteem Table

I was talking to a young lady who was preparing for engagement. By outward appearance she is a "10," but on the inside she says she's a "1 ½." She didn't like herself. She's pressured to be what certain others want her to be, so she had an eating disorder and couldn't stand looking at herself in the mirror. Depression and anxiety problems were created;

being incessantly anxious, she couldn't make decisions. She looked to others to make them for her. All of these problems are produced because of immaturity and insecurity. Insecurities are not what God wants. Insecurity produces fear.

God has not given us a spirit of fear and timidity, but of power, love, and self-discipline (2 Timothy 1:7).

Let's say a healthy self-esteem is a "10" on the scale. If you believed and said, "Man, I'm trash. I'm worthless. I don't deserve to live," consider that to be a "1." We all can see ourselves somewhere on that scale.

The young lady who was to be engaged sees herself as a "1 ½." There's trouble in the making. Think about it. If you only have the ability to care, love, and respect yourself at a "1 ½, how do you love other people? I asked her that.

"How well do you love your soon-to-be fiance?"

"Well, I can love him at a '9'," she said.

Now think about that. If you can only love and respect yourself at a "1 ½," how is it possible to truly love someone else at a "9"?

Some might say, "Well God can help you do that."

God doesn't enable you to do that because your ability to love and respect self is directly related to the ability to give to your mate without taking. What she was really doing psychologically and practically is using the relationship to make her feel better about herself.

We all do that to some degree. I'll go buy a certain model of car because then I can feel better about me. You attach your value and worth to the car. I can attach my value and worth to this particular girl by my side because she's a "ten." Being with her makes me feel better about myself.

I knew a guy who was controlling and manipulative. He had a beautiful young lady friend and he even told me at the end of a session, "I feel better when I'm with her. My friends think I'm 'somebody' when they see this gorgeous woman by my side."

"I advise you never to marry her," I said, "because if she is stupid enough to do that, what's going to happen if she starts putting on a little weight? You see, you're already obsessing about her looking a certain way."

I even told her, "You are foolish to marry this guy, because the moment your body starts changing—and it will—he'll be pressuring you to look like you had when you first got married. You're going to think, 'Wait a minute. He never really loved me. He loved what I looked like.'"

Real or fake?

If I put on the façade of confidence and self-assurance but I'm anything but that inwardly, I am wearing the mask of my false self. I'm not being real with myself, with others, or with life. Why act fake when you can do the hard work of actually becoming confident and self-assured through changing your thought patterns, adjusting your paradigms, and strengthening your faith?

"The model icon of today is Barbie," someone once said. She's the American dream model? Isn't it ironic our icon model today is plastic? Many people today are like that: plastic and shallow. Their goal in life isn't maturity. It's projecting an image to everyone else. We have a plastic society of human relationships in America today. So it's only fitting we have GI Joe out there for the men and Barbie for the women. Healthy relationships go beyond the shallowness. Healthy relationships work past deep hurt and pain into vulnerability and openness.

As an example, if a man were to love his wife as Christ loves His people—the Church—and he couldn't love himself at about a "9," he certainly couldn't love his wife at a "9." He couldn't give to her in a healthy way. Why? Because anything I'm doing in that relationship is taking to make myself feel better, instead of giving to make her feel loved. We will get into the specific dynamics of preparing for and having a vibrant marriage relationship later, but to prepare yourself for a successful relationship with anyone, you must have a true, healthy sense of who you are, your individuality, and the fact that you're different on purpose.

THE OTHER HALF OF THE EQUATION

When you understand who you are, the other essential building block in successful relationships is building up those who you're around. When you become secure in your own identity, you have a powerful tool that few others possess: the ability to encourage and motivate. Why is this such a powerful tool? Because it gives all people what they desperately need: hope and inspiration. It causes people to dream of better things in the future. It causes them to seek the best for themselves and for others.

Listen to the average relational conversation. It's filled with put-downs, insults, and demeaning statements. Why is that? Unfortunately, many people can only feel good about themselves if they are pointing out the inadequacies of another. If you have a healthy sense of self-esteem, you can ignore another's shortcomings and still give a kind, encouraging word to them. Johnny Earl Jones, in his book *You're Gonna Make It: Extreme Encouragement duing Discouraging Times,* said, "To our spirits, encouragement is the air we breathe."

How do you build into someone a sense of value and worth that tells them they are accepted as they are? All relationships are focused on two people having healthy self-esteem. First, we need to know what false self-image is. Someone isn't displaying a healthy self-esteem if they're saying, "You know what? I wish everybody could be like me because if they could, they'd have it all together." That isn't self-esteem. It's a proud, haughty, arrogant attitude, and God despises that.

A healthy self-esteem is when I recognize that I have weaknesses, and I have tendencies to become insecure. There is a great lesson I've learned. Even though I know these things about me, I can make a conscious choice to not allow those things to control me. Through God's wisdom, His love, and His mercy, I have learned what is true about myself, but I'm not going to let my deficiencies define who I am thus they won't affect my relationships and how I treat others. Do those insecurities come out periodically? You bet they do. No one's perfect. But I've learned not to give into those fears that I'm not good enough. I grew up in a home where if you wanted value and worth you had to jump hurdles. And I'm a good hurdle jumper. Because of that, I have two Master's Degrees and a Ph.D., and still want a Law Degree. My whole life has been jumping hurdles to get value and worth.

There was something that changed my life and my outlook forever.

I sensed the Lord saying to me, "I don't care how many degrees you have. You could have none, and I'd still love you just like you are."

"That's hard for me to grasp," I said. "You mean *just* like I am?"

"Yes. Whether you have those degrees or not doesn't matter to Me. Just the way you are, I care about you. Can you handle that?"

"No. I can't," I said initially. "It's outside my understanding to think that you would care for me just like I am."

But when I was able to grasp that His love for me was unconditional, you know what I began to do? I began to build a healthy view of self-value and self-worth. I built it on the person of Jesus Christ and His work and His love for me, and on the Father's love for me. You see, there was nothing we could do to merit God's love. He chooses to love you. So why don't you simply accept that something must be pretty important about you for Him to love you so much He sent His Son to die for you and ransom you back. If you can get hold of the magnitude of God's love for you, not just in your thinking but deep in your soul, that should actually begin to positively change your sense value and worth. When you have a great sense of who you are in God's eyes—as a loved, blessed, and favored child of the King of the Universe—then you are ready to prosper in all your relationships.

* 3 *

HOW TO MAKE LIFE AND RELATIONSHIPS WORK: THE BIBLE AND YOUR BRAIN

My own experience in Christendom is that sometimes we have a tendency to over-spiritualize things about our humanity. God made us. He made the physical body back before sin came into the world. He created each organ to perform its specific function, but he created the human brain so uniquely that it affects every other part of the body in one way or another. I'm going to list the key components of what your brain does, and then I'm going to show you that if you lived according to the Word of God, you would actually make your brain to function in a healthy way. If you don't live out the Word of God, you will actually cause your brain to work in an unhealthy way.

I argue that much of the mental health issues you are seeing today, and the problems inside and outside the church, are due to people not acting on the Word of God. Today, greater than any other time in the history of the United States, more Americans are on antidepressants—approximately one out of three. Part of that is due to aggressive marketing from the pharmaceutical companies, and they do a great job of it. There is, however, another dimension to the problem. Since my field is psychology, I see that the psychological model is used very much like a biological model. In other words, if you're depressed, we treat you strictly as a machine. We are medicating the brain more and more to function in a healthy way, but individuals really aren't doing anything different. People are getting medicated, but they aren't changing the way they act out life. If I am living in sin, and the sin that I'm living in causes my brain to be in a depressed mode, what do I do? I medicate the problem I caused away. Actually it doesn't go away. You just dull yourself to it through the medication instead of dealing with it. We are going to examine the great importance a healthy brain has in your relationships with yourself and others.

Before we look at the complexity of the brain and the ways it helps you function to the utmost when it's healthy, we are going to take a few snapshots of how the brain affects the most vital part of human life—relationships.

Work Relationships vs. Love Relationships

In work relationships, typically there is competition in the work place. You are competing against fellow employees. There's a job position coming available for promotion, and you're in competition with others to get it. Work relationships are designed to be more competitive, whereas, love relationships are supposed to be more cooperative. Sadly, in many marriages there's more competition than cooperation. In the work place there's ambition. We want to provide for the family, make money to get stuff, to develop academically, intellectually, and spiritually, and we want to better ourselves. Work relationships are notoriously distant. You typically don't get emotionally close to people at work. You might share parts of yourself, but for the most part we keep people at a distance. Work is about you and what you can get from your employer and what you can do for your employer. As long as you do something for your employer, you can get something back. At work, you tend to be emotionally guarded.

In love relationships, there has to be mutual concern. There shouldn't be distance; it should involve closeness and affection. It's shouldn't be self-centered; it should demonstrate empathy. What is empathy? Empathy is the ability to feel what another person feels. I usually pick on men because I am one. Men have a difficult time being empathetic, mainly because to be empathetic you have to be in touch with your own feelings. If you can't get in touch with your own feelings and be able to label those accurately, it's much more difficult to help label somebody else's feelings and feel what they're feeling. That's why I love to study Jesus Christ relationally. Jesus was an empathetic individual. The most often phrase used about Him was that He was moved with compassion. Love relationships are about emotional closeness.

Feelings and your brain

There is logic to love. It stems from the human brain. That's the way God wired us. Let's take a look at the way God made us physically, and then relate that to our spiritual growth and development.

Mankind was created to bond. We were created to connect, and we're meant to be connected. There is much research that validates this. For example, there were some studies done during World War II by the Nazis. They took infants, and divided them into two groups. One group of infants was fed, diapers changed, and all their physical needs were met. The other group had their physical needs met, but they also had their emotional needs met—they were held, they were nurtured, they were cuddled, and they were talked to. The group that didn't have their emotional needs met died.

God made us relational. It was His intent from the beginning. That is why He told Adam, "It's not good that you're alone." The Lord is a relational being, and He made us the same way. In the Garden of Eden, all Adam had was God, and God told him it wasn't good. God made us intentionally to need others.

Most people don't think about where our emotions come from—they come from the brain. They are neurochemical processes in the brain. Your brain is an organ made up of billions of cells, but the Lord wired our brains at the biological level so we would need to be connected relationally. You can think with your brain. You can problem solve with your brain. But with your brain you can feel, and you can experience either pain or pleasure.

If my brain is producing more pain than pleasure, I will feel sad, scared, or angry. If my brain is causing those kinds of emotions long term, your symptoms will be unhappiness, fatigue, depression, and you will be closed, guarded, constricted, rigid, and isolated. In order to medicate the pains you carry inside you, you develop addictions or compulsive behaviors.

Compulsive behaviors actually alter brain chemistry so you can change your mood. Did you know if you're feeling down and you begin eating indiscriminately, you are doing it to comfort yourself? Eating releases endorphins in the brain. When those endorphins are released, you alter your mood. The problem with that is when you consistently overindulge and look in the mirror a few days later, you've gained weight. Then you feel worse than you did before. So what do you do to alleviate that pain? Go eat some more. Why? It's a form of medication to you. There are other ways people do this as well. They medicate their brain with alcohol, drugs, or working (workaholism). All these things can alter brain chemistry.

If your brain is producing more pleasure than pain, you will be happy, trusting, and caring. The signs of someone who's experiencing more pleasurable feeling than painful feelings is a sense of happiness, health, energy, well-being, flexibility, creativity, open sharing, responsibility for self, and a capacity for closeness.

In today's culture, 18-year-old to 35-year-old individuals grew up primarily in a divorced home or were raised by daycare or television. They weren't raised by parents; they were raised by someone else. Addictions are preponderant in the families of today. This is not just among "lost" folks. This is prevalent with church-goers also. Just because you get saved doesn't mean you stop drinking, stop looking at pornography, or don't struggle with crack addictions controlling your brain.

Being saved (this is when Christ forgives you of your sins and empowers you with His Holy Spirit) is the first step to overcoming your addictions. You now have the power of God to help you in the process where you didn't have it before. I'm not against any 12-step program, but you can go to a 12-step program to stop drinking and still die and face God's wrath. The power to beat addictions, to live a meaningful life, and to have a clear, creative thinking process comes from Christ. He created us, and He knows how we operate optimally. Today, I enjoy a healthy loving relationship with my step-mother and having practiced forgiveness and seeing reality through an adult mindset, I have found she loved and cared for us all along.

Knowing how your brain works

In everyday practice, we want to know how to control our thoughts, moods, and feelings so we can experience and enjoy life to its fullest. Knowledge is power. When you understand how something works, you can determine how to persuasively use that information for your best, but you can also guard against negative behaviors. We're going to look at the brain, see how it works, and apply that knowledge so we can think and live better.

The brain has a number of different parts to it: the thalamus, the hypothalamus, and the limbic system, but I want to divide it into three main areas. Let's take a look.

The Cortex

The cortex is the frontal part of your brain. This is where all the thinking and judgment comes. All your simple motor skill choices, your ability to think, reason, and make judgments are from that part of your brain. If you've ever seen someone who's had a head injury in the front part of their brain, you'll notice that if the brain stays damaged their ability to think and reason is impaired. They're a lot slower in thinking. Why? Because the cortex gives them this ability. Some might argue, "That ability comes from God." It does come from God, because He made your brain to work that way. It's your brain, whether you like it or not. What keeps your heart going? God does. When He wants to stop it, He will, but the bottom line is your heart does what it does because He made it to do that. Your brain does what it does because the Lord designed it that way. The cortex is the thinking part of your brain. It's not the emotional part of your brain. We'll discover later how you can decide to either allow the thinking part of your brain make rational decisions or succumb to the sometimes whimsical design of the emotional part of your brain.

Your thinking brain is oriented with time. For example, let's say I experienced rejection by my mother when I was a boy. Today I am experiencing rejection from a colleague. I can distinguish the difference between the past and the present. The cortex doesn't superimpose what happened in the past with what's happening now. It can distinguish the difference as two separate events.

The Limbic System

The larger part of your brain which includes the thalamus, the hypothalamus, and the pituitary is the limbic system. This is the emotional part of your brain. All emotions are produced right here. This is also the feeling part of your brain. Brain research shows all feelings come from this part of the brain, and your brain produces all positive and negative emotions. The interesting thing about this research is your ability to feel and your ability to think aren't necessarily connected. Let me ask you this. Have you ever felt angry? Have you ever felt angry and didn't know why you were? You are experiencing it in the feeling part of your brain, but the thinking part doesn't comprehend. It's because they're not connected. But the Lord in His brilliance has connected one emotion with both parts of the brain. It's the emotion of shame. It is the only feeling you can have and know why. You can't walk around having done shameful things and not know why. If you say you don't, I'm going to argue that you're in denial. Shame is such a destructive emotion. God wants you to understand it so you can come to Him for forgiveness before it crushes you.

You can feel angry and not know why. You can feel rejected and not know why you feel rejected. To discern your feelings of rejection requires you developing your cortex, developing your thinking brain so you can make decisions about what you're feeling. The cortex allows you to think things through. Your limbic system is the emotional part of your brain, but it's not oriented with time.

Let's say I was teased, insulted, and ostracized as a child by an individual or a group of people. Those kinds of events create painful memories and are deeply entrenched emotions. Now, if I get rejected today—if someone came up and said, "You're one of the worst teachers I've ever heard"—I have an emotional reaction that pulls up the past feelings of rejection and ostracism. I might superimpose those painful feelings of the past onto the present rejection, and I may even start thinking things like *Nobody likes me. I guess everyone hates me.* Your limbic system is tapping into the unresolved pain of the past. When something triggers your emotional brain, those painful emotions from the past will be unleashed into your thoughts. It can't distinguish between yesterday's pain and today's rejection. It just feels. That's what it does.

One evening my wife and I got into a heated argument, and her train of reasoning and her stubbornness was getting to me (let's leave my own stubbornness out of this).

In the midst of the conflict, I remember a thought came to me that begged me to tell her, "You're just like my stepmother." You see, I had built up a lot of resentments towards her over the years and only wanted to see her as negative.) I could sense the emotional part of my brain urging, "Why don't you share that insight with her. I'm sure she'll enjoy those words." Another consideration came to mind, and I knew it was from my thinking brain. "If you say that, you'll drag this fight to whole new level. She isn't your mother, so whatever you're feeling isn't about your wife. Look at her, Rick. She doesn't look like your mother. She doesn't treat you like your mother did. It would be smart not to say that."

Do you hear the difference between the thinking brain and the emotional brain? This is how the brain works. That's why the Bible has so much to say about your thinking and your brain.

Fix your thoughts on what is true and honorable and right. Think about things that are pure and lovely and admirable. Think about things that are excellent and worthy of praise (Philippians 4:8).

Don't copy the behavior and customs of this world, but let God transform you into a new person by changing the way you think. Then you will know what God wants you to do, and you will know how good and pleasing and perfect His will really is (Romans 12:2).

I have hidden your Word in my heart that I might not sin against you (Psalm 119:11).

So why do you invest in placing God's Word into your mind? It's so you can recall it with your thinking brain. If you develop your thinking brain well, you can manage your feeling brain better.

Understanding Immaturity

Do you know the source of immaturity? Basically, immature people are those who don't use their thinking brain. They let their feelings rule them, and we have a generation like that now. Now I'm not saying that emotions aren't important. You need emotions so you can feel and experience peace, joy, and happiness. With emotions you also feel times of impatience, rejection, and abandonment, but it's at those times you can trust God will reach down, touch you, and help you distinguish what you feel based on truth and reality. Listen carefully though. The Lord won't perform your responsibility for you, so be sure you have developed your thinking brain in order for Him to calm your troubled thoughts.

This generation hasn't been taught critical thinking skills. They haven't been taught how to think through how they feel. Emotions are great to experience life, but they are the shallowest part of the human psyche, and can often lead to flawed thinking if we trust them. In order to train my thinking brain to control my feeling brain, I have to start using it to some degree. Why does it need to be controlled? Your feeling brain is powerful, but it will get you into a myriad of problems if you give into it. Your feeling brain will lead you into affairs. Your feeling brain will convince you to drink. Your feeling brain will cause you to defend yourself when you are totally in the wrong. Your feeling brain will lead you to scream, yell, and insult your mate. Your feeling brain needs to be controlled.

I am not saying you should deny and push away your feelings because that isn't healthy either. What I am stressing is to develop your thinking brain so you'll be able to step back, assess what you're feeling, and then make a decision rather than just give into your feeling brain and possibly act irrationally. By placing the Word of God into your mind—your soul— you'll begin developing thinking skills so you can make healthy choices based on how you feel.

I believe you see Jesus do this in the garden the night before He was to be falsely accused and crucified. During His time on earth, although God, Jesus Christ was also fully man. As He prayed to the Father, His emotional brain was experiencing fear of total separation from the Father when He suffered wrath for the sins of all mankind. In that fear, He requested, "Let this cup (this event) pass from me." Do you hear the feeling brain? All of us would think, *I'm afraid to go to the cross because You are going to reject me and abandon me. I don't want to go. I'm not going.*

But Christ continued, "Nevertheless, not my will, but Yours be done." In spite of how He felt, He made some decisions using His thinking brain. He came to earth to die as a sacrifice for mankind's sin because if He didn't nobody would have hope to escape hell. Christ felt the fear of the coming wrath that was going to fall on Him, but He didn't act according to how He felt. He acted according to what He had decided. During times of hostility against those who call themselves followers of Christ, we must develop a generation of Christians who can use their thinking brain.

The Brainstem

Your brain has a third part. You have the feeling brain, the thinking brain, and the brainstem which is called a survival brain. This is a very important part of your brain even though you are rarely cognizant of it. Your brainstem is attached to your feeling brain and is crucial for your survival. Did you know if your brainstem is dead, you're dead? You can live for a few minutes if your heart stops beating. Clinical death is when your brain is dead.

What does the brain stem do? It's for survival. For example, you're driving down the road and have the green light to cross the intersection. As you're going through you sense an 18-wheeler barreling down on you who had run the red light. Do you shift to your thinking brain and consider, "Oh, look! I'm going to be creamed by an 18-wheeler!" That's not at all what happens. The moment your brain senses danger, your brain dumps epinephrine and norepinephrine into your blood stream, and your heart starts pounding wildly. Without thinking, you slam on the brakes and yank the steering wheel. In this instance, you don't think about the situation—there's no time—you simply react. That's how God wired your brain. It's to keep you alive. Your survival brain operates all the time, constantly scanning the environment for a sense of threat. If you feel like someone's about to attack you or reject you, your brain senses that rejection or pain and starts doing something to protect you.

Emotions and the brain

The Word of God is very clear. If you obeyed the Word of God, you would cause your brain to function in healthy ways. If you're consistently opposing the Word of God, you'll create pain, hurt, guilt, and shame. Did you know that Adam and Eve had no guilt, shame, nor fear before the fall? Their brain didn't have to produce it. After Adam and Eve rebelled against God's commandment, the first two emotions that sin produced was fear and shame. Adam never knew these emotions before, but when he sinned, he said, "I was afraid," and he also went into hiding "because he was naked." There is the fear and the shame. Now every human being has to struggle with these sins until the day they die, some varying in degrees than others. Depending on how well you use your thinking brain based on the Word of God determines the level of fear and shame you'll have to deal with.

The first two emotions Adam experienced at the Fall were shame and fear – painful emotions. Sin did that for us, and we have Adam to thank. But the everyday responsibility for our individual life is still ours. When you experience a painful emotion, you do it yourself. When you insult your spouse, you create pain for yourself, whether you like to admit it or not, and because you are a Christian, you should feel guilt. God wired you that way, and the guilt you're feeling should motivate you to do something about that sin. If I confess and ask for forgiveness, my brain produces gratefulness for the forgiven debt. When you refuse to reconcile because of pride and won't admit your sin you will keep all the guilt, pain, and fear.

That is the reason more and more people are on medication. We have a generation who has grown up with so much pain from dysfunctional families, broken marriages, and broken families, and then they get married and produce even more pain through their own marriages. They had a measure of pain when they went into these marriages and create more with conflict born of past hurts. I argue that the Word of God is clear on relationships and our way of thinking. If I'd experienced pain or rejection in my past from parents who were terrible role models, and I keep hanging onto anger, resentment, and bitterness, I won't mature emotionally or relationally. I can't get anywhere with my relationship with them as an adult because my stuffed hurtful feelings are affecting me, not them. Forgiving them would free me and my brain to experience God's joy, peace, and blessing again.

How do you know if you have peace in your mind? You feel it. How do you know if you have joy, or anger or bitterness? You feel it. What's fascinating is during a PET scan, you can actually see the energy produced by different parts of the brain depending on which part of the brain is doing the thinking. One patient was struggling with extreme anger, and through the scan you could see the energy emitted by his limbic system— his feeling brain. If you give into that anger, it becomes sin because you act out the thought mentally or physically. In order for this man to avoid making a wrong emotional choice, he had to move his energy from his feeling brain to his thinking brain. After five minutes of intervention to control his anger, he began to think rationally, and in the scan you could see the energy moving to his frontal lobe—his thinking brain. The Lord wired us wonderfully, and His Word works directly with the way our brain operates. If I'm going to be angry and not sin, I need to be in control of my brain and I better be able to use the correct part of my brain. If you don't act on the Word of God to make your brain work in a healthy way, you'll be on medication like so many others. Now I'm not saying there aren't some chemical or biological processes in the brain that would breakdown. Just like any other organ, it can breakdown, too. For most, the guilt, shame, anger, and fear that are caused in life come from problems you make, and your brain will react to those things so you will act to correct them. If you experience continual mental pain and hurt, you're dealing with them in the wrong way.

As a Christian, if I want to live out the abundant life Christ promised, at some level my brain will be producing the feelings of abundant life, which are the fruits of the Holy Spirit. You'll know if you have the fruits of the Holy Spirit in your life because you'll feel them, and you'll feel their effects. *The fruit of the Spirit is love, joy, peace, patience, gentleness, goodness, faithfulness, kindness, and self-control* (Galatians 5:22-23).

You might ask, "Are you trying to say if I live according to God's Word I won't experience pain?" No, that's not so. You are going to feel pain, but depending on what you do with the painful things that happen to you will determine how long you stay there. I can stay in depression and blame people all day long, but blaming won't help me. It will keep me in my pain. If you grew up that way, you don't have to stay that way. Once you are born again, you can go to God for help. "Lord, show me in Your Word what I have to do differently. Teach me what I need to learn. Forgive me for my sin and my sinful attitudes. Help me to forgive others who have wronged me as you have forgiven me for my sins." If you don't like the mental pain you're going through, develop your thinking brain by incorporating the Word of God into your thoughts. Don't be conformed into the mold of this world (which takes no responsibility for personal thoughts and actions, and blames everybody else for their hurts and wrongdoing), but be transformed by the renewing of your mind. The Lord created you and your mind. Why not read the owner's manual (the Holy Bible) so it can work at its very best?

* 4 *

THE ART OF INTERACTING

All healthy relationships are based on two people having a healthy value and healthy sense of self-worth. The lifeblood of healthy relationships are encouraging words and attitudes. No matter what kind of relationships you're engaged in, if they're peaceable and friendly they're more enjoyable. The main problem between any couple, group, or work force is that each individual "brings to the table" his own opinions or presuppositions about what he should do and what you should do. Often times those views don't agree, and when two or more try to enforce them conflict ensues. From this point voices raise, arguing begins, and anger envelops the atmosphere. The intelligent conversation of rational people mutates into exaggerated bantering that produces nothing.

It's as common as grass to find people who won't agree on various subjects. Mature people can work through the differences though. Relationships that work have individuals who care about others more than desiring to justify their own opinions. Someone who's consumed with his wants, his rights, and what should be owed to him will soon find himself without an audience to hear him.

Selfishness and selflessness are two side of the same coin. Negativity and encouragement are the same way. What do I mean? Everyday we have a choice to make. The Lord has blessed us with a brain and a will, and He expects us to use them. So when we walk into the day, the things that happen around us shouldn't determine what kind of attitude we're going to have. You have the ability to choose your attitude before the day even begins, and when unfortunate or frustrating events occurs you'll be ready to overcome them instead of them overcoming you.

Remember the choice you make for yourself will also determine how you interact with others and how they'll reciprocate. You are the coin. On one side you can have a "chip on your shoulder," "wear your feelings on your sleeves," or just be a "sour sad sack." The other side of the coin is your decision to be joyful, friendly, and winsome.

Think of the science projects you did in grade school using magnets and metal shavings. When you used the positive side of the magnet and placed it on the bottom of a sheet of paper, you could get the metal shavings on the paper to follow your magnet around. No matter where you moved the magnet under the paper, the shavings would gather and follow. When you flipped the magnet over and used the negative side, it didn't matter how close or how often you'd try to get to the shavings they'd always be repulsed. Now, consider your attitudes as the magnet and the metal shavings as the people in your life, be it at home, work, or church. What kind of attitude would you like to own? It's your choice. A negative attitude drives people away. A positive, encouraging soul invites people into his presence without even a word.

There's nothing that maligns and kills relationships more than a critical, bitter, negative spirit. People can sense a negative person instantly, and they'll scatter like a school of fish at a shark's approach. Being around a person with a negative attitude is like standing in the presence of someone who never brushes his teeth: you try to be nice, but there's no way to hide that something stinks.

The reason why encouraging, positive people team with friends and acquaintances is because others feel better about themselves through their example and kind words. We all like those kinds of people, and we may even aspire to be a positive, friendly person, but for most the problem is that they don't know how.

Read this next portion alertly. There's no way we can speak encouraging words or perform friendly actions unless you are secure with who you are. Everybody around us is insecure in one way or another. People are drawn to folks confident in themselves, and there's only one way someone can truly be secure. Confidence in life can only come through a relationship with the Lord Jesus Christ. Yes, that is correct. I'm not talking about religion. When I'm referring to your relationship with Jesus, I'm talking about being forgiven of your sin and having your guilt removed. I'm referring to being loved unconditionally by the Creator of the Universe, and knowing He cares about you and He's is in control of everything. Your real self-worth and self-value comes from what All-knowing God thinks about you, not what flawed, fickle people think about you.

Remember, being confident in life doesn't mean you've mastered every aspect of your life. Having a healthy self-esteem means you can be realistic about yourself without putting on a façade.

"Hey, I've got it all together," someone might say. "I've got it made." Some of us don't actually say those words, but we live as if we do. Have you met people like that before? Do you try to convince others that's the kind of person you are? When we're honest, we know we don't have it all together in all the situations of life. That's living in a mirage, an illusion. Healthy self-esteem is when I recognize that I have weaknesses and that I have tendencies to be controlling, manipulative, and insecure. When I admit these things about myself, I begin escaping the prison of meeting everyone else's expectation of me. I begin to accept the fact that I can change and that I don't have to be controlled by my fears and insecurities. But it's not until I admit them to myself that I can truly change. I won't let my quirks affect me or my relationships with those around me. Do they come out periodically? You bet they do, but I've learned to not give into my insecurities that say, "I'm not good enough."

God loves me. For many years, I couldn't grasp that concept of unconditional love, but once I was able, that knowledge built my self-worth and my self-value. I had to accept that something must be pretty important about you and I for the Father to love you so much He'd send His Son Jesus Christ to die for you so you could live forever. When I realized God's love and understood my worth based on who I was in Christ, I understood God had given me an incredible power: the ability to encourage and shore up individuals around me. The ability to encourage and build a sense of value into other people is a gift everyone admires.

Here are several important scriptures that are keys to building, preserving and enhancing your friendships, work relationships, and your personal interests:

- People with good sense restrain their anger: they earn esteem by overlooking wrongs (Proverbs 19:11).
- Loyalty makes a person attractive (Proverbs 19:22a).
- A person's words can be life-giving water: words of true wisdom are as refreshing as a bubbling brook (Proverbs 18:4).
- Your own soul is nourished when you are kind, but you destroy yourself when you are cruel (Proverbs 11:17).
- A relaxed attitude lengthens life; jealousy rots it away (Proverbs 14:30).
- A gentle answer turns away wrath, but harsh words stir up anger (Proverbs 15:1).

The art of interacting involves making others feel like what they've got to offer is important, and if you're a good listener you'll find it is. The language of today is sarcasm. Sarcasm is a language lined with little daggers. It never encourages. It never promotes healthy relationships. Positive interaction leaves people you talked to realistically feeling good about themselves. There's something affirming to say about everyone if you're careful to look for it. We're going to look at four tools which will construct esteem in your friendships, work relationships, and your marriage. The key to start these tools correctly is putting the emphasis on esteeming others instead of manipulating people to build yourself up.

Tool #1—You need to accept the other person unconditionally. Total acceptance is the most important foundation in building esteem in relationships. Without it, your relationships rest on the shifting sands of emotions.

A great example of unconditional acceptance is found in the 8th chapter of John's gospel. In this scenario, a group of religious folks drag a woman caught in adultery to Jesus. They interrupt Jesus' teaching as they accused the woman and prepared to stone her. Curiously, when Christ turned, He didn't address the sinful woman, but the mob of self-righteous men.

Jesus understood she was an adulteress, as did everybody around him. And yet He gave her unconditional acceptance. He never said a word about her sins. However, He did confront the hypocritical religious guys whose hearts were full of sin even if they didn't show it outwardly.

"Who do you think you are to stone her? Any of you guys who've never sinned cast that first stone."

They dropped the stones and walk away leaving her standing in the classroom Jesus was teaching in. Everybody watching saw Jesus living out the love and forgiveness He'd been espousing to them.

He looks to the woman and asks, "Woman, where are those condemning you?"

"There are none."

"Then I don't condemn you either."

That is the level of acceptance you must show your mate, your friends, your associates. No matter what they do extend unconditional acceptance. Your colleague might have blown a deal both of you'd been working long and hard. Your spouse may have burnt the dinner or forgot to put the toilet seat down. You don't have to accept the action, but separate that incident from the person and accept them unconditionally. When people know they are accepted as individuals it takes the performance pressure off them.

Acceptance gives them the freedom to fail, but more importantly, it gives them the desire to do their best.

We've talked about owning our own self-value so we can be beneficial to others, but it would be a travesty to steal someone else's value. Jesus said it like this, "Do for others what you would like them to do for you" (Matthew 7:12). Some people have nicknamed the Lord's saying "The Golden Rule," and how precious it is for someone in authority, position, or persuasion to esteem another as someone special. So never, ever let anyone tear down your sense of value and worth, and certainly don't do that to someone else.

Tool #2—Put the past in perspective. Each person hopes for respect in the present even if they've had an imperfect past. All of us have a history, some more menacing, some more embarrassing, and some downright shameful. Everybody knows what they've done in the past, but nobody needs to be reminded of it and accused because of it. Holding the past over someone's head doesn't exercise Tool #1 in building esteem in relationships; it destroys.

You wouldn't want to be reminded incessantly about the mistakes you've done. We regurgitate those enough on our own, bringing embarrassment by the mere memories of those past actions. You struggle with your own past as do others. Put the past in perspective and thank God for how far you've come. When you consider someone else's past, appreciate the work the Lord is doing in their life also. Even as a Christian, we make mistakes and fall into sin, but we don't have to stay down.

I love the phrase by Sy Rogers. He says, "Salvation is not immunity from our humanity." Most of us like to live as if when the Lord saved you, He wiped away your past. Wouldn't that be nice? There's a promise from God in 2 Corinthians 5:17 about your past which says, "Therefore if any person becomes a follower of Christ, he is a new person. They are not the same anymore, for the old life is gone. A new life has begun!" Jesus forgives us for the past guilt, shame, and sin of our old lives. He gives us a fresh slate and continual forgiveness. But don't misunderstand what this promise says. The Lord didn't wipe away our past; he cleansed us of the filth of past sin. When you were redeemed by Christ, your soul was bought by Him, and your destiny is abundant life and your destination is heaven. But along the way we must realize humanity is still a part of you. The baggage and residue of the past may still be with you. That's why you must put your past and others' pasts into perspective. You're not going to be perfect, but give others the freedom to experience the process of growth, as you would want others to do the same with you.

You're not going to be free from your past because your past is part of you, and it leaves residue even though you've left it behind. We all have residue. Some people show it more than others. Some hide it better than others. But it's there. Salvation isn't immunity from humanity. But by being born again, you have the spiritual power that allows you to initiate the process to deal with the issues of the past, learn from them, and put them in perspective—specifically God's perspective. When you view your past through God's eyes, you can work through the issues and over time they will no longer control you.

What about another's past? Many people today come from broken homes where abuse, neglect, alcoholism, drugs, and other painful experiences and traumas were present. These traumatic experiences or ongoing anxiety provoking patterns develop defensive reactions in a child that assist in one's ability to survive in the midst of the craziness. We take these life experiences and defensive reactions into our adult life and are usually not aware that we are being affected in the present by the pains of the past.

Never assume you're interacting with someone without a past. We all have a history, and we all struggle with different things from day to day. Dr. Herb Reavis, Jr. once said, "Be kind to everyone because you never know what they may be going through."

Tool #3—Plant positive words. You know the old saying: Sticks and stones may hurt my bones, but names can never harm me. That's not true at all. Scripture says in your words is the power of life and death. It's not just in the words you say, but it's often the words you don't say. When you don't say, "I care about you and what your going through," "I appreciate your loyalty and your friendship," or "I love you," you could be holding back vital words someone might need. Everyone needs acceptance, approval, and appreciation. Approval and appreciation is expressed verbally. You just have to say it. How often have you been thankful for your friendship, or your spouse's sacrifice and hard work, or your child's respectful attitude but just failed to tell them? That's the only way they'll know. Encouraging words build a person's self image, and it's my privilege and responsibility to have those words readily available. Even if I'm angry or not getting my way, I have the choice to dismiss negative feedback and instead bless someone with positive words. If I want to bless someone and build their sense of value and worth, I speak positive words. If our Heavenly Father were here physically, those would be the words He'd speak. So why not practice the blessing of being one of His mouthpieces and cause positive words to become your new language?

Tool #4—Constructing in difficult times. Weathering the storms of life by turning to each other for strength and encouragement will build a relationship. If you learn to communicate and deal with the storms together as a team, you build a sense of confidence in one's self, but also the attitude that *we* can overcome. *We* can beat this thing.

The normal reaction during tough times is to reject and blame the other person. Surfacing in conversations are phrases like "You're just like your mother," or "This must be from the baggage you have from your first marriage." That's not turning toward each other. That's rejecting and isolating your partner. Two things that build intimacy are physical closeness and emotional openness. If we don't weather the storms and do good construction in difficult times by using good communication skills and problem solving skills, you actually affect your mate's self image, value, and worth in a negative degree. You will also be affecting yours because you'll sense, "I can't do this," and "How come we can't work through this." We want to build a sense of worth that says, "We are a team, and we can get through these difficult times together."

Allow the freedom to fail. Release your mate from the prison of performance with the freedom to fail. Can you fail at something and not be a failure? Of course, you can. What's the difference? Your attitude is the difference maker.

Somebody interviewed Thomas Edison and asked him how many times it took him to finally develop a light bulb. He admitted it was over a thousand times.

The interviewer asked, "What was it like to fail a thousand times?"

"I never failed a thousand times," Edison said. "It was just a thousand tries that didn't work."

He never saw the attempts as a failure; he just saw them as possibilities he could rule out. Was it frustrating for him? Sure. But the difference between a failure and someone who fails is that a failure quits, while the one who fails learns what doesn't work and tries again, never giving up.

* 5 *

BUILDING RELATIONSHIP BRIDGES

When you build a wall, you want to keep somebody out. In Germany, when the Berlin wall was built, it separated free Germany from Communist Germany. It kept two different ideologies distinct, but it severed relationships between the people on each side of the wall. Since suspicion was fed, people on one side of the wall feared the other and hostility brewed. Fear builds walls, not bridges.

When you build a bridge, your goal is to connect two things that are separated by a gulf. In the United States, we have chasms, mountains, rivers, and bays that divide one piece of land from another. In order to get to the other side quickly, easily, and without destruction, a bridge is built. These bridges have often allowed us to see loved ones who were in otherwise impassible regions. Bridges create connectedness. In relationships, there are different bridges that need to be built to get to normally barren and impassible territories in another's life caused by fear, disappointment, or broken trust.

Understanding

The first structure to build the bridge is the foundation. In a relationship, understanding the other person is foundational. When you're open to get to know the other person, you build a bridge that tells them, "Hey, this guy really cares about who I am." When you take time to see where a person's coming from instead of condemning them for how they are now that they're here, connections begin to be made. Remember, just as it takes time to build a bridge over a chasm, it takes time and effort to create a sturdy relationship with somebody else.

Trust

The next process that goes into building an unshakable bridge is establishing the trusses. The trusses are the girders or framework for supporting the actual bridge crossing. Trust is the truss in the bridge that holds the relationship from falling apart. Without trust, you don't have strong relationships. Today, many are skeptical about trusting anybody, and too few are actually trust worthy. That's why this country is rampant with so many shallow people, shallow relationships, and shallow churches. People want something to believe in, something to invest their life and energy into. Trust is taking your life and investing it into someone else, believing they will mean as well for you as you mean for them.

Love

After the foundation and the trusses are set up, it's time to lay down the bridge crossing. This is the part of the bridge people enjoy the most because it involves them the most. This is the passageway for the vehicle called connectedness. Whether it's romantic or dedicated love in a marriage, sibling love, family love, compassionate love, or love for your friends, this is the part of the bridge that we recognize as what closes the gap between individual lives.

Bridging a natural separation

Why is it necessary for us to know how to bridge the gap in relationships? The gap, the isolation, is real. Everybody is insecure about themselves in one way or another. Different people just deal with it in different ways. Some get aggressive and pushy. Others turn docile and reclusive. A number grow busy and become overachievers. Still others are outgoing but never reveal their true self.

When you seek to understand someone else you take the emphasis off yourself and direct it toward someone else. Who are the least pleasant people to be around? Self-centered folks. Contrariwise, who are the most enjoyable? People who consider others more important. When you become a student of who someone else is, you are relating to them their importance as a human being.

When you establish trustworthiness to another, you are telling that person, "What you share with me, what you say to me, and the relationship we are building are safe from harm and disappointment. When someone builds trust, they are destroying doubt and building faith. They can know you won't undermine them, talk badly behind their back, or deceive them. Suspicion is a natural human response, but establishing trust shows you are genuine and caring.

The Bible says the greatest thing of all is love. Love brings comfort, peace, and pleasure. Relationships without love are simply noise without any substance. Every human wants to feel loved, and the greatest expression of love was shown by God Himself when He sacrificed His own Son to free us from the shackles of sin and give us a life where we could express our love back to Him.

People are complex. We each have different personalities, temperaments, and past experiences that mold us into who we are and how we think. With that knowledge as our springboard, what are some of the factors to look for and expect in different people so we can bridge the gulf and build strong relationships in families, friendships, and work environments? If we understand people, build trust, and display love, we'll construct bridges into others' lives. If we reject folks because of their demeanor which was created by past decisions and circumstances, we erect walls of fear and distrust. We are going to look at the different factors.

Factors hard to change in a person

There are certain relationship-hindering or relationship-damaging factors in a person's life that is difficult for them to adjust or change. They may be hard to change, but not difficult. Now there are several avenues in which we can address this issue: Am I the one who has these problems? Do I have a relationship with a loved one or an associate who can be difficult to deal with? Am I willing to have the patience with difficult people to get the best out of that relationship?

Here are some relationship factors that could be hard to deal with, whether they're your own or those of someone else:

Controlling

Some people have a tendency to react strongly or defensively to problems. If you know of a person who has an explosive personality type or know someone who's manipulative, deceitful, deceptive, or controlling these people are basically insecure and afraid of letting anyone know their real "self" for fear that people might find a scared little person who's frightened of being disrespected or abused. In that state, don't expect close or trustworthy friendships. If you're dating someone like that, don't expect them to change just because you get married to him or her.

Insecurity

On the basic level insecurity is a difficult factor to change, but never impossible. It's said that in one way or another, everybody is insecure. This is a valid statement since nobody knows the future and nobody knows what's in another's heart. A sense of insecurity may always be there, but the question is, "what are you going to do with it?" I've learned not to give in to it. It is a choice you make. You don't have to be a victim of your own thought life. You are the master of your own thoughts. And what's the key to conquering your thought life? Rely on supernatural purpose and power. Paul the Apostle said, "…I keep working toward the day when I will finally be all that Christ Jesus saved me for and wants me to be…Forgetting the past and looking forward to what lies ahead, I strain to reach the end of the race and receive the prize for which God through Christ Jesus, is calling us up to heaven" (Philippians 3:12-14).

Past hurts

Overcoming the pain, heartache, and disappointment of past relationships can be difficult to overcome. Once again, this can be hard, but it's not impossible. Being assailed or hurt by someone who doesn't like you can't begin to compare to the heartache caused when a close friend or loved one abandons, neglects, or tries to destroy you. The reason why it's so hard to change the callousness and suspicion that clouds your thinking is because after a relational tragedy like that you're unwilling to let anyone close to you again. Walls are up; bridges have been demolished. The good news about hurtful relationships is that you can use those experiences as a testament of the trials you went through to attain your victory over those debilitating emotions.

Stepfamily complications

Having children from a previous marriage can also cause some friction and anger when working in other relationships. Mixed families have an array of challenges, but they aren't challenges that can't be overcome. For children, the rearranging of authority figures, clashes in parents' ideologies, and new environments can lend a lack of stability. It's hard to flourish in your gifts and your abilities when you are clinging for security. For parents, the disharmony between differing ideas of running the home and raising the kids can become a war of wills. And, of course, friction at home inevitably leads to frustration and conflict outside the home, straining work relationships and hampering friendships. Second marriages fail at a rate of 68%. Unfortunately, this holds true across the line for Christian marriages as well. The reason for that typically is because of the conflicts concerning raising the children. Stepfamilies are not God's ideal, but that doesn't mean they cannot be wonderful healthy families. Stepfamilies themselves are born out of loss. There was either a death of a spouse or the death of a marriage. With the emotional challenges connected with stepfamilies this can sometimes be difficult to handle.

Religious differences

Differing religious backgrounds can often create contention in relationships. Conflict in this area usually results when one person tries to argue why his religion is valid, defending against the other who says it's not. It is improbable to argue anyone out of what they believe. Religious views for many are lifestyle choices. To argue with what they believe is to say their lifestyle is insufficient. As Christians, we aren't to argue with anyone of differing religious persuasions, but instead we are to lovingly share truth, and let what we talk about be lived out in our lives.

Definitely avoid bickering about preferences between different Christian denominations. Doing this in front of people who don't believe in Christ gives them the impression that we're not unified and contentious. There is a time and a place to talk about religious or denominational differences with a humble attitude.

Money problems

Money crises in your life can be hard to change in an individual. If you lost your job, your source of income, all your relationships would be strained. Getting in debt and being in debt will also challenge your relationships because of the stress and anxiety involved. In this case, you need to adopt a new mindset about spending and saving. This subject is so important because many friendships, associations, and marriages are destroyed because of financial difficulty. To give a token solution in this one paragraph would be to understate the issue. If you or someone you know has money difficulties, I'll refer you to www.Crown.org or books by Dave Ramsey, *The Total Money Makeover* and *Financial Peace Revisited*.

Factors you can change to improve relationships

Communication and conflict resolution skills

Learning communication and conflict resolution skills are keys to improving relationships. There will be times when you'll have disagreements and misunderstandings. Without wise response and discernment, conflict can quickly escalate. When confrontation arises between people, the primary weapon used is a sharp tongue which leads to negative styles of talk-fighting with each other. Arguments rapidly become negative words, put downs, or the silent treatment. If your emotions guide you during these times, you can expect escalation because your emotions are the shallowest and basest part of your soul. When you're being led by the Holy Spirit, you'll bear the fruit of the spirit: love, joy, peace, patience, kindness, goodness, faithfulness, gentleness, and self-control.

If you see this as a need, seek out wise and experienced Christians and ask them for their advice. They will love to share and pour their life experiences out to you. The greatest treasure of wisdom we have are the godly elders of our churches who have lived through life's experiences and mistakes and can tell you what works and the attitude it takes to be successful.

Successfully handling disagreements

Working relationships are the lifeblood of team environments. Handling disagreements is paramount. In a team atmosphere, personal preferences should be sidelined for the good of the bigger entity. Remember, a team is a collaboration of different personalities working toward a common goal. Whether it's a football team or a marriage, the collective goal should be the good of the team, not bending to the whim of an individual at the detriment of the bigger purpose. The Biblical mandate is to die to oneself in order to allow for unity and harmony.

Problem solving

In every relationship, there are important issues that need to be addressed. When all parties come to an agreement when differing issues surface, they will prevent contention. Harboring different attitudes about important things causes confusion. If disagreements erupt, all involved should agree to be responsible enough to address the problem with maturity. Next, the disagreement must be identified. Sometimes, people don't even know what they're arguing about because the difference is so vague and amorphous. A problem is half-solved just by successfully defining it. Once the problem is clearly identified, then the procedures to put aside preferences for the good of a greater cause can occur, and the problem can be solved. This works in business, friendships, and in marriages.

Realistic beliefs about marriage

Marriages are the bedrock of all relationships, but in this all-important union between two different individuals there are differing expectations among spouses. For example, one spouse may think romance should always be part of the marriage, while the other thinks marriage is a joint venture for them to dutifully impact the world. It is important to remember that because the other spouse doesn't think about the marriage the same way you do doesn't mean they don't love you or hold the relationship in high regard. Each spouse needs time and must make time to become a student of the other. True joy in the marriage doesn't come when you manipulate your spouse to do what you want. Real marital peace, joy, and harmony comes when you deliberately plan on blessing your spouse or being a blessing yourself. When you choose a selfless, kind, and happy attitude toward the one you married, your spouse will desire to reciprocate in a way that's pleasing to you.

Handling attitudes about important things

Whether it's a team, a business, or a marriage, there are important things which need to be addressed. Who is the best one to make the choice on what's important? Can anyone give input? There are people who are better at different things than others. On a football team, a coach can see the full scheme of the offense or defense where a player concentrates solely on his position and those opposing him. In a business, the one who calls the shots has the education and experience to steer his company through good times and bad. In marriage, one spouse may be more adept at raising the kids while the other is skillful in handling the finances. Before starting anything great, you have to predetermine what's most important for you. In Stephen Covey's book *The Seven Habits of Highly Effective People*, he stresses that one of the tools that keeps an entity focused on what's most important is having a "Mission Statement." A mission statement is a concise description of what your marriage, business, or team stands for. When you know what you stand for, you know what's most important.

A personal story of relationship bridge-building

This is a story of an every day morning in the house with the wife and family. Observe how seemingly meaningless words and attitudes can escalate into misunderstanding then conflict. Also, mind how relationships can be healed after the connection is broken.

One morning I was coming down the stairs, feverishly putting my tie on, and looking at my watch. I was running late. My oldest son was in the 5th grade, and he was sitting at the breakfast table with the rest of the kids.

"Go ahead and start eating," I said.

My wife tells me, "Slow down. Those people will wait for you."

"No they won't," I said, "because we're running late." I turned to the kids and said, "Just start eating."

"I'll say the blessing," my oldest son says, not because he's so godly, but because he's figured out that if he says the blessing we get done quicker and eat faster. So he quickly says the prayer.

I've been observing this behavior for quite a few months and decided that for our family devotion time this particular morning, I'm going to address the real meaning why we ask a blessing over the food we eat, and do it in a very loving way. We eat breakfast, push the bowls, milk, and cereal to the side, and I look at the kids.

"Instead of doing our normal devotion," I tell the kids, "I'm going to ask you a question. Why do we say a blessing before we eat?"

The kids look at me confused. My wife glared suspiciously.

"Think about it. Did you know that nowhere in the Bible does it say you have to say a blessing? It doesn't. As a matter of fact, it doesn't say whether you have to say one before, during, or after or even if you do say one."

"But we will say it," my wife said. "And we'll say it before the meal."

I look at her, thinking *stay out of this.*

Turning back to the kids, I said, "People are taught rules, but they aren't taught principles. We teach rules, but we don't teach principles behind the rules. Every rule has a principle. You know a rule: pray before your meal, but do you understand the principle?"

The kids just stared at me.

"I want to teach the principle. If you learn the principle, it becomes part of you, not just something you do. I want you to understand the heart of the rule, not just the law. It's the difference between being genuine and being a Pharisee.

Kids, right now all this food is right here on the table. How does that make you feel?"

"Thankful," my little daughter said.

"Good answer," I commended. "Do you know right now in our city there are kids that don't have any food on the table? They will go to school today without any food. How does that make you feel for them?"

"Sad," they said corporately.

"What is that sadness going to prompt you to do?" I asked.

They started throwing out ideas, all of which revolved around how to get food to those who don't have any.

"Oh, good ideas," I said. "Do you see? Sadness prompts you to do something. Godly sorrow prompts you to change, to go do something."

I then asked, "Well, how does it make you feel that we have food then?"

"Thankful," one said.

"Grateful," answered another.

"Now, who gives us the food?" I asked.

"God," they said.

"Are you sure? So you're grateful that God gave it?"

"Yes."

"So you don't say a blessing just because that's what you're supposed to do. It's done because of your sense of gratefulness."

"But we will say it before we eat," my wife piped in.

I looked coldly to her and wanted to say, "Stay out of this. This has nothing to do with you right now." But wisely I didn't. I started back with the kids to reiterate the principle to insure they understood.

"But we will say it before," my wife demands again.

Now I'm mad. I turn to the kids and instruct them, "Get up. Go get ready. We'll be leaving in 5 minutes." Once the kids cleared the kitchen, I turned to my wife. "I'm angry with you."

"I know you are," she said. "But we will say a blessing and it will be before we eat."

"I'm angry at you because you're undermining me," I replied. "I'm trying to teach the kids a principle about why we do something, and all you worry about is some stupid rule."

Leaving her in the kitchen, I went back upstairs, got my stuff, and began walking out the door.

"I'm sorry," she said.

"Thank you," I replied as I reached for the door handle.

"You're not thankful," she accused.

Now I'm really mad and slam the door closed. The Lord was actually giving me the opportunity to practice this principle He had shown me just recently. That's the way He is. He teaches you something, but He doesn't want you to just know it, He wants you to live it out. At that moment I didn't seize the moment. I walk to the car thinking, *I am mad right now, but I refuse to go to work mad, especially since I just learned this principle about relationships.* I turned my eyes heavenward. "Lord, I have no idea what her problem is, but personally I want go back in there and just lay into her. She has no right opposing me. Where is this coming from?"

I sensed the Lord asked me, "How long have you been a spiritual leader to her?"

"Only the last two or three years," I said, but at this point we'd been married for 14 years.

"Do you think she trusts you yet?"

"No sir."

"Do you care?"

"Yes sir."

"Do you think she might still be afraid to trust you right now?"

"Yes sir."

"That's where the opposition is coming from. So why don't you go back in there and minister to the fear *that you created* and I will deal with her sin."

I went back into the house and said, "I need you to know that I don't appreciate you telling me that I'm not thankful when I really am, but that doesn't solve the problem. However, the Lord has shown me something in my walk back in here. I realize that I have failed you as a spiritual leader for many years in this marriage and it's hard for you to trust me. For the last two or three years, I feel like I've been consistent, but I realize that you still don't trust me. I want to earn your trust because I love you, and I don't want you fearing, because I want to be there for you even in the spiritual relationship."

I hugged her, kissed her, and walked out the door.

If I didn't seek to get at the root of the problem (which, to some might seem petty and insignificant, but to the matters of the heart are important), then I would have been ruled by my pride and selfishness, and the results would have been negative. If I would have left with our differences unresolved, I would walk away with guilt because the Lord would say, "What are you doing?" When I chose to listen to the Lord and be obedient to Him, put aside my own self-centered arrogance, and love and respect my love more than myself, I walked out with this great peace in my heart, and I literally sensed the Father say, "Good job. I'm proud of you, son."

When I was responsible for obeying the Lord even when I didn't feel it, I was freed from guilt and freed from the pressure caused by the rift in the relationship. What I experienced is what all people look for: peace of mind. That peace of mind comes only with a clear conscience before the Lord. But I gained something else as well. Because I decided to build a relationship bridge instead of a wall, I was able to begin developing a pathway of trust. An hour after leaving the house, my wife called me and asked me to forgive her for the way she handled things that morning.

"You've already been forgiven," I said. "But thank you for calling."

Relationship bridges happen when we discern the needs of others, understand those needs, and then try to meet them. By doing this you're investing in another's life, you bless your own, and you please the Lord God Almighty.

* 6 *

ACCEPTANCE AND SECURITY

No one is an island, and no one is self-sufficient.

Who knows you deeply?

Who knows you better than anyone else?

God knows you better than anyone else, and He accepts you unconditionally. He accepts you just the way you are; He just doesn't want you to stay that way.

But we need to feel more than God's acceptance, don't we?

The Lord knows that as well. He desires a relationship with us, but He has created us so that we weren't meant to be alone.

In the very beginning of time, the Lord brought this to mankind's attention. *And the Lord God said, "It is not good for man to be alone. I will make a companion who will help him." So the Lord God formed from the soil every kind of animal and bird. He brought them to Adam to see what he would call them, and Adam chose a name for each one. He gave names to all the livestock, birds, and wild animals. But still there was no companion suitable for him.* (Genesis 2:18-20).

When the Lord marched out each species of animal, Adam gave them names to identify them, but He noticed something common among those creatures—they came to him in pairs. Each pair complemented the other, one male and one female. It became quite obvious to Adam that as a human, he was alone.

You don't know what you're missing sometimes until it's brought to your attention. In the beginning of creation, Adam had enjoyed his fellowship with God, probably never realizing he was lacking anything. The Lord knew what Adam needed though. Mankind needs God more than anything else, but the Lord knew that people need other people as well.

So the Lord God caused Adam to fall into a deep sleep. He took one of Adam's ribs and closed up the place from which he'd taken it. Then the Lord made a woman from the rib and brought her to Adam.

"At last!" Adam exclaimed. "She is part of my own flesh and bone! She will be called 'woman' because she was taken out of a man." This explains why a man leaves his father and mother and is joined to his wife, and the two are united into one. Now, although Adam and his wife were both naked, neither of them felt any shame (Genesis 2:21-24).

We weren't meant to be alone. God made us to be social creatures. We desire to be known. God made you to know Him, and for someone else to know you.

In order to build an intimate relationship and to create an atmosphere of acceptance there are three concepts we must ingrain into words, actions, and attitudes.

Caring

When you are dating, you do a lot of things to get to know your potential mate. You call them during the day just to ask, "Hey, how are you doing? What's going on with you today? Oh, things are going rough at work, why don't you tell me about that?" Right now when you date, you want to know what's going on with your "special someone." You care about what's important to them, and what's important to them you make important to yourself. You long to know their deepest thoughts, dreams, and desires. When you care you make time to learn about the other person, sometimes putting important things on the back-burner to gain as much knowledge about them as you can.

Now let's fast-forward ten years into an average married life. Odds are that you won't even ask that question once that year. Why? Because somewhere along the way you quit trying to gain their acceptance and you ceased accepting them as a valuable part of your life. You could care less if your spouse shared about what was happening at work. That's what's happening in America right now.

Spouses tend to stop talking and asking about how the other person is feeling and trying to know about each other. Instead, when they do talk it's to get something from the other person. Don't believe it?

Throughout years of marriage counseling, I have come upon one question that seems to dominate the "cooled off" marriage relationship. And the reason for it is because couples stop being intimate. They stopped trying to know each other deeper. They allowed disappointments and hurts—intentional and unintentional—to callous their hearts and allow the feeling of love to "die on the vine."

What's the question? Let's say you call your spouse after ten years of marriage where the intimacy has worn off. What's the first question your spouse is going to ask?

"What do you want?"

Isn't it a shame that two people can slip from knowing what they want—they want to know each other—to saying, "What do you want?" Somewhere along the way you stop caring, your world turns inward, and you don't even wonder how the person you used to care about more than anyone else is feeling.

The Lord is our greatest example. He never stops caring about us. His love for us never wanes. He never secretly thinks anything bad about us. He always wants to know how you're feeling. He wants to deeply know us, and He does because He created us, but He wants us to desire to know Him intimately.

Sharing

As I use this word, I am not talking about sharing physical possessions, money, or property. I'm talking about something infinitely more valuable—sharing your innermost self with your spouse.

Let's say your spouse came up to you after a long day and asked, "Honey, how did things go for you today?"

Your response is, "Uh, all right."

Do you think your conversation or your relationship is going far if you don't open up and share? This means to disclose some thoughts and feelings. In Proverbs 23, the Bible says God is intimate with the upright. He discloses Himself to the upright. The greatest form of self-disclosure God ever did was when He left the praise and adoration of heaven to come and dwell among mankind. *And the Word was made flesh and dwelt among us...* (John 1:14). He who was unapproachable approached us to give us hope. He revealed Himself to us so we could know the only one who could give us hope.

If you want to know something about your spouse, what do they have to do? They've got to share what they think and how they feel. This is to vulnerably disclose, to make one aware of what's going on inside of you. So if you and your spouse want a healthier relationship, you'd be wise to keep caring and to better disclose yourself.

Here are some examples of how to damage your intimacy, your feelings of closeness, your "**Us-ness**":

Let's say your spouse can sense something's bothering you and asks, "How are you feeling right now?"

"I'm okay," you reply.

You're lying, and your spouse isn't fooled. What would keep the line of communication and the emotional doors open would be to let your spouse know what you're thinking or struggling with.

If you're not careful and caring, look at the dangerous turn this can take. Let's say your spouse asks what's wrong, you make yourself vulnerable by sharing, then your spouse says, "Oh that? You just need to get over it. That's life."

Let's say my spouse responds that way to me over and over. Once again my spouse might ask me, "How are you doing?" What would be my answer? Would I be vulnerable and share how I feel or what I'm struggling through? Of course not. If my spouse responds to my self-disclosure that way, we're not going to get close. My response would be something like "I'm doing fine," or "It was a good day."

If you show you don't care about what your spouse's feelings, you won't build an intimate relationship. Where there is no emotional sharing, there is no relational or loving growth.

Acquainting

The third concept we must internalize and practice is that of acquainting. This means to make familiar. In Psalm 139:3, the Bible says, "You know my path and my lying down, and are acquainted with all my ways." It's a synonym for "intimate" that speaks of beneficial giving or caring involvement. Basically, this verse says God is caringly involved in all your ways. Do you ever wonder why He does what He does for you? It's because He's caringly involved. He blesses you, supplies for you, and walks beside you always because He cares for you.

Why would I want to know my spouse? I care about my spouse as an individual.

Why would I disclose to her? I care about our relationship.

Gaining a strong relationship comes when you become motivated about acquainting yourself with your spouse. Hopefully this won't come as a surprise to many, but your spouse is different than you. Your mate has a different background, different upbringing, different experiences, and a different personality. God made us that way. Here's where the relationship turns sour: when we look at the differences as problems instead of possibilities. Larry Burkett once said, "If two people are alike in a marriage, one of them is unnecessary." Instead of arguing over differences in personality, why don't you explore this deep person you've chosen to spend your life with? Become acquainted with all the things that make your spouse different, and you may find that they have attributes and abilities that can add to the success of your relationship when coupled with yours.

Some of the biggest intimacy needs

Acceptance

Whether people want to admit it or not, we all need acceptance. It's one of our biggest intimacy needs.

When I was doing a marriage conference in South Carolina, I said, "Everyone in this room needs acceptance."

One lady raised her hand quickly and said, "I don't."

"You don't need anyone's acceptance?" I asked.

"No, not from anybody."

"So, you don't need acceptance from God?" I asked.

"Well, I guess I do need acceptance, don't I?"

God made us to need acceptance. Acceptance means receiving another person willingly and unconditionally, especially when the other person's behavior has been imperfect.

In John 8, we read about the woman who was caught in the act of adultery, and who was dragged before Jesus by members of the Sanhedrin who demanded her death. She had sinned and was guilty of death because the law called for it, but the Lord gave her unconditional acceptance even though she didn't merit it. He didn't condone her actions, but He forgave them, and showed her He accepted her as a person. He met that need.

We have that need. We can meet others' need for acceptance, and there are so many ways. We can show affection through kind words, caring deeds, and closeness through physical touch. We can show appreciation by saying "I love you," by expressing thanks, and through praise and commendation. Recognizing accomplishments and effort, showing approval, and affirming somebody is important in relationships.

Attention

We all have a need for attention. Attention is conveying appropriate interest, concern, and care. We can do this by taking thought of another and entering their world. No matter how calloused someone might act, that person has a need for attention.

Here's an example of meeting that need: Let's say you were thinking about your spouse and instead of just letting those thoughts pass you decide you're going to call them even if they're at work. "Hey honey, I was thinking about you just now, and I want to say hi and see how you're doing."

By doing that you met a need for attention even if you or your spouse realizes it or not. It shows you were taking thought of them.

Years back, I instructed a men's class, and I taught them about meeting their wives need for attention. I told them, "When you call your wife, she may ask what you want because she's not used to you calling without demanding or instructing. When you do call, she isn't used to you meeting her need for attention. I challenge you to call during the day. Everyday, I call my wife while I'm at work, and I don't ask for a thing. I call to meet her need. It only takes ten, fifteen, or twenty seconds. 'Hey how're you doing? Are things going rough with the kids? Anything I can do to help? I was just thinking about you and wanted to let you know I love you and care about you.' I don't ask for anything because it means so much more when you call and invest your time into a priceless relationship."

One of my guys took me up on the challenge. He was a truck driver who'd been married for about twenty years. "I took your advice," he told me. "And it got me in trouble."

"What do you mean?" I asked.

"I stopped in a hotel for the night, and I got thinking 'bout what you said. I decided I'd do that phone thing, and I called home."

Now remember, the trucker didn't have a pattern of calling his wife.

"I wanted to meet that need for attention," the trucker continued, "and I said, 'Hey honey, how are you doing?'"

"Fine," she answered. "How are you?"

"I'm good. I was thinking of you and realized how much I love you and thought I'd call and share it with you."

"All right, tell me," she said suspiciously. "What did you do wrong?"

"It got me in trouble," he told me. "I can't do that again."

"No, you keep it up," I encouraged him. "She's not used to you showing care and meeting her need for attention. The more you do it the less suspicious she'll be and the more excited she'll be to receive your calls."

Isn't it a shame that in relationships—and this is indicative of many marriages—that we lose a sense of meeting these needs for attention?

Security

What a great human need this is. Security has nothing to do with whether you have deadbolts or security systems in your home. It's all about whether you feel safe in a relationship, both physically and emotionally.

Some of you grew up in a home where you weren't sure how the parent or step-parent was going to act or what they might say from day to day. If you shared something, would they accept you? You could feel a sense of distance developing in a relationship like that. When you have a degree of aloneness and where there is a lack of trust, there will be insecurity. Unfortunately, that insecurity can also be prevalent in a marriage relationship.

God didn't design us to live in insecure relationships. Security means harmony in the relationship. When I go home, I shouldn't be worried about whether my spouse is going to yell at me today. I shouldn't have to wonder if my spouse is going to respond to me or not when I come through the door. That's an insecure relationship. We need security. Men need security. Women need security. It is each individual's responsibility to assure their relationship is free from harm.

Support

This simply means to come along side and gently help with a problem. Here's a caution. Support doesn't mean you barge in and try to solve the problem; you're there to help them come to a solution. Individuals need to know they can achieve victory over what they're struggling against, but they also need to know we're there to cheer them on and shore them up when needed.

"I don't have these needs."

Everybody needs these things. There may be some macho guy out there who says, "Not me. You may need those things, but I don't because I'm a real man." There may be some overconfident woman who says, "I am a self-made person. The only thing I need is me." You are actually in denial.

The American icon male are people like John Wayne, Clint Eastwood, and Christian Bale. Do you realize the attitudes of John Wayne and Jesus aren't compatible? Jesus and Eastwood or Bale don't match. Those people who are just actors representing a role they played have become the model of how guys should be. They're tough. They're unmoved. They're loners. They show no emotion.

Christ Jesus was also tough. He was authoritative, and He was a leader. Jesus, however, showed compassion for people, He forgave them, and He patiently taught scores of folks. He was always around people, and wherever He went there seemed to be celebration. Above anyone else, Jesus was a real man's man.

Men today have been socialized tough and austere. Take the example of a three-year-old boy and a three-year-old girl. They both fall down and skin their knees. We know they have a physical need—to address the wound. At that moment they also have some intimacy needs. They need comfort. They also have the need for attention, a sense of "Do you care that I'm hurting? Do you care if I'm bleeding?" This addresses the emotional area of their lives. Both children need attention, both need comfort, and if the parents did those things, they would be providing security and support to their hurting kids.

But in reality, here's what happens. When the little girl falls and hurts herself, we meet the need for attention by picking her up and saying, "Oh no, you're hurt. Honey, let me see what happened. I'll clean that up for you, and you'll be just fine." She walks away feeling loved, accepted, and cared for.

The little boy, same age, has the same accident. He too has needs for attention and comfort, but after he hurts himself, you look at him and say, "Suck it up, son. Be a man!"

Is it any surprise we have two generations of disconnected men? They have been taught from an early age that if they acknowledge they have needs they're weak. The Lord created us with those certain needs and has given us the privilege of meeting each other's needs. Men have denied others from ministering to those needs in the name of tough manhood. But when those needs go unmet, it creates pain in the human experience. As you grow and mature you will fix that pain in one way or another. You will find a way to medicate the pain. You may even deny it exists, saying, "I ain't hurting. I don't need anything." But you're lying to yourself when you say that. We all have needs, and when you try to fix the problem yourself by finding ways to make up for those unmet needs, the solutions aren't healthy—you become a workaholic, get addicted to drugs, alcohol, sex, pornography, or even isolate yourself.

What's wonderful is that the Lord wants to meet our needs. He wants to heal our broken hearts. He's able to calm our troubled mind. He loves us, directs us, supports us, comforts us, and never secretly thinks anything bad about us.

It is the job of the husband to be thinking in those terms when your wife is troubled and needs to talk to you.

"I just don't feel like things are going the way they should be in our relationship," she says. Don't you realize the underneath the statement she is trying to find a sense of security?

I could say something loving like, "I think it's just fine, so why don't you get over it." Will that create security for her? No, it'll create more insecurity. Don't be surprised if your sex life isn't that great. "Well, you just act like a log," you say to her. Why wouldn't she? The relationship isn't free from harm, and you're part of the problem because of your insensitivity to ministering to her need.

If you want your spouse to think healthy and have a positive mental behavior, meet her needs. If you refuse to they will experience painful feelings of unworthiness, insecurity, anxiety, condemnation, bitterness, and hurt. That will lead to disrespectful behaviors, including playing communication games but it could lead into harmful results such as addictions, compulsions, and self-abuse. In the long term, these behaviors result in a dysfunctional family, poor self-image, personality problems, and depression.

What we receive from our spouse is what we sow into their lives. If you plant good things in their thinking, you'll receive good things. If you sow negative, abusive things, you'll receive something that will bring you disappointment. The choice is yours.

For men, this uncaring attitude began when they were young. Parents somewhere back in the past decided that they didn't care enough to minister to the needs of their boys. We have a generation of men who were insensitive and uncaring to their boys, so is it any wonder that we have a generation of men today who are uncaring to their spouses? You can track the problems of all society right to the breakdown of marriage. Around 65 BC, the Roman philosopher Cornelius said, "The foundation of society is its marriage."

If you want a healthy relationship that is long lasting, you must think in terms of meeting needs. Everybody wants their needs met differently. For example, my wife is not keen on affection. She likes it, but it doesn't speak to her needs being met. I never grew up with affection, so I love it. I like affection. When she meets my need for affection, I feel loved. If I show her affection she'll be thankful, but it's not as fulfilling for her. She needs support. If she asks me to do something and I do it, she feels loved and cared for. It took me a while to figure this out, but now I know real joy and harmony in the relationship comes from meeting your spouse's needs. My job isn't to minister to her needs the way I want to minister, it's to minister the way she needs them met.

* 7 *

CONNECTEDNESS NEEDS

Are you single or are you alone?

Every single person has an idea of what the perfect marriage should be like. Some singles can imagine paradise without being married. But whether it's with friends or with a wife, people need to feel connected.

When talking about the idea of connecting in the human experience, your brain will do one of two things. You will either experience pain or you will experience pleasure with it. You decide which way your brain goes based on what's happened to you in other relationships.

Intimacy is a sense of connectedness or bonding that tells you that we are close. If two people are going to connect, it does have pain because to bond with someone would require some painful things to happen in the relationship. It requires two people with two separate agendas to die to themselves, so they can live with one harmonious purpose. Before people get married, they should count the cost of the freedoms of ideas and activities you may have to forfeit. Before the vows are ever stated, serious thought should go into what happens beyond the wedding ceremony. Ladies, going to mom about every conflict in the relationship will only complicate matters. Men, hanging out with the fellas for some late night male bonding times several nights a week at the softball field or at the club will only cripple the relationship. What you do with the pain of bonding will either keep you in pain—which produces bitterness—or it can push you back to a sense of pleasure. It's all in how you evaluate the pain of change.

I do a "design your own paradise" exercise often at conferences I do around the country. A while back, I was in Detroit, and was talking about designing my own paradise. "My paradise," I told them, "would be on the Blue Ridge Mountains in a 4,000 square-foot log cabin with stone fireplaces. I'd have my computer and my favorite computer games, and all of my Civil War and World War II books (I'm a big history nut). I'd drive a Dodge Ram pickup truck with extended cab, big wheels, roll bar, lights, and a wench on the front." I relayed this in a church in Detroit and the whole place went quiet. I thought, *Well, that's interesting. They aren't listening.* At the first break of the seminary the pastor walked up and said, "My whole church is employed by Ford."

Now I understood why they didn't appreciate my paradise.

After the break I went back in and said, "Actually, I like Ford F-150's better."

Hypothetically, let's say you get to choose your ideal paradise. Here are three things you can choose to make your own paradise: first, you get to choose where or what your paradise would be. Would you select the mountains like the Rockies, Blue Ridge, or the Smoky Mountains? Would you pick an island such as one in the Bahamas, Costa Rica, or Hawaii? Or would you choose a spacious home, or a high condo with a great view?

Secondly, you get to choose what kind of stuff you want there. Would you decide to have plenty of good food? Would you bring a Frisbee, or golf clubs, or mountain-climbing gear? How about hobbies like electronic chess, macramé, or free weights to work out with? Would you like to have a sports car, a yacht, or a camper?

Third, what would you do there? Would you relax or train to run a marathon? Would you want to hunt, fish, or grow your own garden? Would you want to snow ski, surf, or hang glide? Maybe in your paradise you'd like to do a lot of traveling.

So if you could design your own paradise and I allowed you to have these three things—and they must not be conflicting with each other— would you take it?

Oh, by the way, there are some stipulations to your paradise. The first non-negotiable is you get the paradise your way, and you are in charge. Would you still take it? Sure! That sounds pretty good. I would get my mountain cabin, my truck, my Civil War books, my computer, I'd go hunting, I could do whatever I wanted to do, I could travel around, and I can do all that and be in charge.

Secondly, not only do you get the place you want, the stuff you want, get to do what you want, and be in charge, but you are with God in all His love and majesty. Would you take it?

But let's say nobody else is allowed with you. Now would you take it? Did you just hesitate on that answer? Imagine you're where you want, with what you want, doing what you want, and you're in charge and the King of the Universe is with you. Does the feeling of not having another person around sound lonely? You won't be alone; you're with God. Think about that now. Would you take that paradise? Do you sense a stirring inside you that says something isn't right? Do you feel a sense of conflict inside you? We all want to be with the Lord when we go to heaven or when He returns to end all of pain, time, and sin, and comes to bring His children home, but in our human existence it feels unnatural not to have any other human around. Why? It's because you weren't designed in such a way.

What you have just experienced was the scenario the first man Adam was in. God created the earth, and put Adam in the Garden of Eden and gave him authority over the entire earth. Could you imagine being commander of the entire earth?

Adam had a perfect environment. He was living in his paradise. There was no sin, no anxiety, no taxes, no terrorism, there were no crashing planes, there were no cars breaking down, and there were no women. He was in the perfect environment, and it was stress free.

Not only did he live in the perfect environment, but he possessed everything. He possessed everything because God made it and gave it to him. The Lord might have said, "Hey Adam. It's yours, and you get to manage it however you want. You get to name the animals, and what you call them are their names forever. You have my favor, blessings, and love. And if you need more I'll provide it for you." God placed Adam in an exalted position. Everything obeyed Adam from the house cat to the

Siberian Tiger to the Nile crocodile to the Great White shark. He was commander-in-chief of all of God's creation.

Adam also had a dilemma. After giving everything to Adam and giving him rule over everything, the Lord introduced a crisis into Adam's thinking.

What was the first crisis in all humanity?

"It's got to be when Adam sinned in the Garden of Eden," you might answer.

That was a crisis, but it wasn't the first one.

"It was separation when God forced him out of the garden after sin."

That was horrible but even that wasn't the first crisis. Adam's first crisis was when he realized he was alone. When you're in a perfect environment, and you're with God, and God shows up and tells you something is not good, would you agree you have a problem? The Lord told Adam his problem was he was alone.

"I've got everything I could want," Adam might explain. "All my needs are met. I'm in charge of it all. I can do what I want with it. And now Lord, You're telling me it's not good because I'm alone?"

Adam thinks about it for a moment. "Okay, so it's not good that I should be alone. Lord, can I ask you a question?"

"Sure Adam."

"How can I be alone? I am with You."

In Genesis 2:18, the Bible says, "And the Lord God said, 'It is not good that the man should be alone; I will make him a help suitable for him.'"

Adam heard that but he had no idea what it meant, so the Lord created an exercise for him which would enlighten him. Adam knows he's alone because God told him he was, but he didn't know what that meant. In Genesis 2:19, God instructed Adam to start naming all of the animals, so that's what he starts doing. The creatures pass in front of him two by two. "Bear, Mrs. Bear," Adam declares. "Dog, Mrs. Dog. Hippopotamus, Mrs. Hippopotamus."

I almost imagine at some point Adam would ask, "Lord?"

"Yes, Adam."

"You know I'm naming these animals like you wanted me to, and it's kind of a neat venture, but something's missing."

"Well Adam, what is it?"

"I don't know. I can't put my finger on it."

Psychologically, Adam is fully human like you and I, just without sin at this point. He's no different than we are. He's made in the image of God, and we're made in the image of God. Just because you have sin in your life doesn't mean you're not made in his image, it just means your relationship with God is broke. I think Adam, from his emotional side, starts to sense something isn't right. Finally, the scripture says that through the animal naming process Adam comes to a realization. Every animal kind was a pair, but there wasn't another like him. What do you think Adam felt the moment he realized there wasn't another like him? He felt alone. Deeply alone. God told him that, and he didn't understand. Now he knew what was meant because he was experiencing it. There is a principle you see throughout scripture. Whenever God taught a truth, He made you experience the truth He just taught you. The reason He does this is because although you know truth, doesn't mean it translates into your experience. The Lord doesn't want a bunch of "eggheads" with a skull full of facts but who don't know how to make an impact with the revelation He's given them. There are a lot of people who know about God's Word and who know about love, but they aren't experiencing it. What good is knowledge if it doesn't affect your heart and positively change your relationships?

Have you ever felt alone before? There are couples who've been married for many years who go to bed next to each other, turn their backs on each other, and who never touch, because in their marriage they're deeply alone.

I know single people who don't feel alone. God didn't say it is not good for a man or a woman to be single; He said it's not good that they're alone. Aloneness has nothing to do with marital status. It deals with whether your heart is connected relationally to God and to others.

I believe the issue of aloneness is the problem for all mental health issues. There are children today growing up in broken homes. The parents don't love each other, and the kids grow up with a deep sense of aloneness where they're disconnected from their parents—the ones who're supposed to be modeling how relationships work. Is it any wonder why this generation doesn't know how to relate to each other in a healthy way? Have you ever thought you could be in a football stadium with thousands of people and still be very much alone?

There are lots of people trying to deal with their aloneness needs by getting married. It doesn't work. Others try medicating their loneliness with drugs, alcohol, pornography, and overeating. In its simplest truth, the feeling of aloneness loses its grip when you know the Lord loves you, when you understand the spiritual gifts He's given you—these spiritual gifts are clues to your inclinations and preferences in relating with folks—when you take your attention off wanting your selfish desires to be satiated—dying to your self—and when you make meeting the needs of hurting and lonely people a priority in your life. Loneliness fades when you are helping others instead of wondering why everyone's not giving their attention to you.

Adam now knows what it's like to be alone. He knows what it's like to not be connected with other people. God puts him into a deep sleep that would change his life forever. The Lord took out one of Adam's ribs and created Eve. In Genesis 2:18, the Lord promised Adam He'd make a helper suitable for him. Adam, not doubting that God would carry through with His promise, simply assumed He'd do it, even though he didn't know how. The Lord ended Adam's aloneness by delivering his wife, Eve, so that now he could have a right relationship with God and with another human being. Whether you're married or single, when you have a growing, healthy relationship with the Lord and with other people, you won't suffer from the affliction called aloneness.

Body, Soul, and Spirit

When God created us He made us body, soul, and spirit. He also made us needy. Most of us today, especially men, don't like to admit that we're needy.

You may have met somebody who is a spiritually strong person with the attitude that says, "I don't need anybody. When it comes right down to it, all I need is God."

Wow! What a spiritual giant. I wish I could get to the point where all I needed was God. I've got one problem with that theologically. If that is true, you'll have to explain why it wasn't good for Adam. At one point all Adam had was God, and the Lord said that wasn't good. Can you explain why it's sufficient in our fallen state to only need God when it wasn't good for Adam in his non-fallen state? The Lord created us in our natural state to not need His relationship alone. You might argue, but if God decided to make us needy—to not need Him only, but also to need others—He can do that. He intended us to need Him and also need others. Now let's talk about the needs He's given us for our body, soul, and spirit.

Body needs

Your body needs are your physical needs. You need food, sleep, water, air, shelter, and clothing. You *need* those things. What happens in the human experience is if these vital needs aren't met, you'll die. If you don't drink water, eventually you'll die. If you don't eat food, eventually you'll die. But here's the key point of everything we're going to learn about all of our needs—if the need aren't met, something is going to die.

Spiritual needs

Each individual has spiritual needs, but what are they? We need communion with God. We need a relationship with the Lord. These are spiritual needs. Note this: if you don't get your spiritual needs met from the true God, you will get it through totem poles, various religions, idolizing material goods, worshipping sports, or any other countless ways. You will display your spiritual need to worship something. You need a relationship with the Lord Jesus Christ because you need freedom from guilt and shame. Thus, you need confession and forgiveness. Those are spiritual things that you need.

What happens if those needs are not met in the right way? What happens if you choose to neglect your Creator and worship something or follow a belief that's not consistent with Who He is? The Bible says your greatest need is redemption—to be rescued from the wrath of God because of sin, the influence of the devil who wants to condemn your soul, and the power of sin which will only lead you down a pathway of destruction. Redemption means to buy back or to ransom. Jesus came to save us by purchasing our soul by exchanging His to take the punishment we richly deserved and to free our souls from the control of sin and Satan.

Now you're probably thinking, "I'm a free-thinking, free-talking American citizen. I don't need to be purchased because I'm not in slavery to anything."

Everything in life has spiritual ramifications and spiritual influences. Because we're all born sinners, the Bible says we have a wicked spiritual father called the devil. He wants nothing more to destroy you physically, and divert you from believing in Christ so he can see your soul destroyed for eternity. That's why you see so many addictions, so much sin, and so many contradicting religions. Your enemy the devil has a full repertoire of counterfeit ways to get your spiritual needs met.

You don't believe it?

Let me give you an example. If I have hunger, which is a human need, I can feed it with something. I could eat rat poison or I could eat a hamburger. Both will solve the need for hunger, but one will kill me while the other one won't. The same is true in the spiritual sense. You can worship a totem pole all you want, but it is like eating rat poison—at some point you will die with no hope.

Christ Jesus said, "I am the way, the truth, and the life. Nobody can come to the Father except through me" (John 14:6). Jesus said He was the only Savior. The Bible says that since we are born into the family of Satan we must be "adopted into the family of God." That's why Jesus said, "You must be born again" (John 3:3). He is the One who loves your soul. *"For God so loved the world that He gave His only begotten Son that whosoever believes on Him will not perish but have eternal life"* (John 3:16). Why worship something or follow a belief that will not satisfy or give you hope for eternity when you can repent, believe and have a relationship with an All-powerful God who loves you and wants to rescue you?

Soul Needs

What is a soul? The soul is your mind, your will, and your emotions. We relate to the outside world through our body using our senses. It is with your soul that you relate to God. The Lord speaks from His Spirit to your soul. He may use His Word, but He is still speaking to the spirit inside you. He may speak to your soul using another person's words. He can speak to me through my circumstances. He's God, and He can choose to speak to me as He sees fit, but He's never speaking to my physical senses. He's always talking to my spirit and my soul.

It's with the soul we also relate to other people. Have you ever seen two people talking about a subject you didn't think was important, but watched them get emotional and hug each other because of the information shared? They are communicating their soul needs to each other. These are things we can't understand with our senses. They can only be perceived and appreciated with your soul.

Your body, your spirit, and your soul have needs. When the needs are met, there is life. When they're not, something dies.

* 8 *

FORGIVENESS IS CRUCIAL

The most vital ingredient for any human relationship is forgiveness. You may have been taught this in church as a religious concept. Religions do talk about this, but it isn't strictly a religious concept. The Lord commands us to forgive, but even non-religious people can understand and practice this with each other. The difference between saved folks and non-Christians is we have a motivation to forgive that they don't. Who can you not forgive when the Lord has forgiven you by paying the penalty for your sin that He didn't have to pay? He chose to suffer the wrath of the Father so you could be forgiven. Remember, forgiveness is something we select to do. Nobody can earn our forgiveness or it's not forgiveness at all—that would be called paying a debt.

Taking a storyteller's view, we are going to look at one of the greatest accounts of forgiveness from John 8, and we'll see just how we can apply it to our relationships with each other.

Picture yourself walking with Jesus down the slopes of the Mount of Olives early in the morning, mist rising from the ground and the grass still wet with dew. His strong, steady pace quickly brings Him into the city, and with kind intensity in His eyes, you can tell He is about to change somebody's life today.

People are already gathered in the Temple and the courtyard, eager and hungry to hear the gracious words to come from this man's lips. He talked of God, His kindness, and His mercy; the people pack in closer, hearing words of hope they'd never heard from the religious leaders of the Temple.

As Jesus was teaching, He heard shouting and ruckus in the background. He continued to teach and each individual stayed transfixed, but the noise grew louder and headed in the direction of the Master. Jesus raised His hand to signal He was going to pause His teaching, and He turned to the sound of angry voices and the whimpering of some young lady they're dragging along with them.

Some of the bearded, scowling men spotted Jesus and pointed His direction, then they thrust their way through the crowd and shoved the woman into the open area in front of Jesus. "Teacher," they addressed the Lord, "this woman was caught in the very act of adultery. The Law of Moses says to stone her. What do you say?"

Jesus looked to her. She was bowed down and unable to lift her eyes, He senses the emotions she's experiencing: shame, embarrassment, fear, and even anger. Anger? Yes, because it takes two to be caught in the sin of adultery. Where was the man involved? *Why were they picking on me?* She probably wondered. *Why am I being singled out?*

The religious leaders, the Pharisees, wanted to destroy Jesus with the answer He would give, but they had no problem destroying anybody else along the way to get to Him. So here she was, helpless and guilty before King Jesus. The Lord, instead of answering their question, noted a spot of dust on the ground, bent down, and started doodling.

Pastors will speculate He wrote all kinds of things, but the scripture doesn't say anything about it. As Jesus drew on the Temple floor, the religious leaders kept pressing Him for an answer. Why didn't Jesus say something profound that would blow their minds? After all, He was a great master communicator. There is a strategy in communication. When someone wants to exploit you, they don't care what you have to say, they just want to trap you, and that's what the religious leaders were trying to do with Jesus. All-knowing, all-wise Christ Jesus discerned the trap they were trying to lay. So as they continued to urge Him to answer, He remained silent and didn't even acknowledge them. In moments, He turned the situation on them. In their frustration and disappointment over not being able to trick Him, and being awed by His patience and self-control, their attention was turned fully to Jesus. Now they weren't testing anymore. They really wanted to know what Jesus had to say.

When all was silent and all eyes were on Him, Jesus stood up and looked the way of the leaders and said, "Any one of you guys without sin, throw the first stone at her." Then He bent back down to finish the dust picture He was drawing.

In the dead silence, the sharp clacking of a stone falling to the stone floor echoed in the temple. Another follows. Then another. Soon it sounds as a small storm of stones hitting the floor. The only noise to follow is the sound of awe through the crowd, and the shuffling of the religious leader's feet as they exit Jesus' presence.

There in the silent room was Jesus, a throng of onlookers, and a woman who was either naked or barely dressed since she'd been snatched from the act of her sin. She had sinned. She stood there in shame, but she didn't feel fearful anymore. Everyone there knows she's an adulteress, but in the presence of Jesus she felt an unconditional acceptance. Why would He defend her, knowing what she'd been accused of?

Jesus stood and turned to her. "Woman, where are those who condemn you?"

With tears in her eyes, she excitedly turned to the Lord, wondering why such a godly man as He didn't disapprove of her. "There are none, Lord."

"I don't condemn you either," Jesus replied. "Go and sin no more."

When you ponder the sin the woman had committed during that era, do you think the religious leaders had a right to stone her? They knew they had the right to stone her. Jesus knew they had the right to stone her. The Pharisees were referring back to a passage in the Mosaic book of Leviticus which demands the punishment of death for the sin of adultery. They not only wanted to condemn her, but they wanted to condemn Jesus, and they were going to use their trick question to destroy Him and her no matter how He answered.

If Jesus had said, "You can't stone her," He would be denying the authority of the law which He had said He'd come to fulfill. Why? He was a Jewish man, and the responsibility of the Jew was to obey the law. He couldn't just ignore the command in Leviticus.

But if He would have answered differently by saying, "Okay, go ahead and stone her," He would have put Himself in serious trouble because the occupying Romans were the only ones allowed to actually execute anybody. So if Jesus had answered that way, He'd be subverting the earthly governing authority.

He understood what they were trying to do, but understand, when He said, "You without sin cast the first stone," He was acknowledging their right to stone her. This is the key concept to understand about forgiveness. When someone hurts you, wrongs you, or offends you, the world's standard says you have the right to 'get back' at whoever sinned against you, either through retribution, bitterness, or separation. The things your parents might have done wrong to you in the past deserve repayment. Being hurt by an ex-mate, an employer, a fellow employee, an old boyfriend or girlfriend, or an old friend may have caused you to think it requires justice.

Forgiveness does none of those things. Bitterness and anger toward someone strips you of peace of mind, and it distorts and poisons your personality, not to mention souring the relationships of everyone else involved with you. Forgiveness is crucial to restoring your own self back to some level of health emotionally and spiritually.

So what's the definition of forgiveness? Forgiveness is ceasing to feel resentment toward an offender or giving up demand for justice or retribution. Forgiveness is giving up the right to hurt someone back. It allows for the possibility of healing in a relationship which will create greater intimacy.

The Pharisees knew they had the right to stone the adulterous woman, and so did Jesus. He said nothing about their right; He asked them about their eligibility. Jesus could have said something like this: "Guys, I agree with you. I know you have the right to stone her, because I'm familiar with the passage in Leviticus. Before you stone her, I have a question for you. Though you have the right to stone her, who among you is eligible to stone her?"

Now that's a different question. People will hurt each other, incidentally or purposefully. Folks may wound each other, or mates may wrong each other. If you are human those things are going to happen. The question is not whether you have the right for retribution for wrongs against you, but are you eligible to throw the stone? The answer is no, but we go ahead and throw the stone anyway.

The Lord acknowledges your right for retribution and vengeance. He doesn't question the right, just the eligibility. According to scripture the only one eligible is the one who has no sin.

Now you find yourself in a quandary. Let's say my spouse hurts me. I have the right to 'get back,' but I'm not eligible because my life is not sinless. But what about the injustice that's been done to me? There's been an offense. What do I do with my rights? This is where it gets hard and interesting. The Bible says, "Vengeance is mine, says the Lord. I will repay." But if I can't repay because of my sin and He can, what do I do with my rights? I have to give them up to the One who is eligible—to the One with no sin. The Lord knows how to repay perfectly where we don't. The Lord is also merciful to me and to others. Think about it. If you do something wrong, you want mercy. If someone else does something wrong, you want revenge. The Father knows how to implement justice. Yet in so many relationships, individuals hang on to their resentment, their bitterness, their rights for vengeance and retribution because they want to get back at someone for what they did.

Forgiveness is the process of cancelling the conditions of the mind that prevent the full flow of love and vitality through a person as a result of a life event. In this sense, it is not an external act of pardoning, it's not a forgetting of the lessons learned, it's not permitting oneself to be overridden, it doesn't stop one from taking appropriate wise action; it's an act of self-care.

Before I get specific into what forgiveness is, let me tell you what it is not.

What is not forgiveness?

Forgiveness is not forgetting

You've heard people say "Forgive and forget." If you don't forget it, does that mean you don't forgive it? If you were ever sexually abused, is it possible to forgive the offender? Sure it is. Do you ever think you'll be able to forget what happened? Unlikely. Forgiveness has nothing to do with remembering. And just because you remember an event doesn't mean that you haven't forgiven it. Now I will say that if you keep bringing it up, that may be evidence you haven't let it go. Forgiveness in and of itself doesn't mean you forget what happened.

Forgiveness is not reconciliation

Forgiveness doesn't always repair a relationship. Forgiveness is meant for one person. It was meant for you. It was meant for me. It's an act of self-care. Forgiveness is not about a relationship; it's about me. Can I forgive an offender? Yes. Does that mean the offender will want to have the relationship restored? Not necessarily, because forgiveness isn't determined by reconciliation. Forgiveness is a choice I make. Can you forgive someone you don't trust who's wronged you? Yes, but it doesn't mean you have to try to be their friend.

Reconciliation is a relationship issue, and it takes the cooperation of two people to perform it. If both of you want reconciliation for the way you hurt each other, then it will require practicing confession and forgiveness in your relationship. If you confess what you did wrong and forgive when the other person hurts you, you will restore yourself and the relationship. By doing this you'll strengthen and restore the "Us-ness" to your relationship.

Forgiveness doesn't perpetrate injustice

You don't use forgiveness to allow a person to keep hurting you. If someone hurts you and you forgive, only to have the person hurt you again incessantly, you can forgive, but you aren't required biblically to stay and keep receiving abuse. If I forgave you for a wrong you did to me, it doesn't mean you are relationally healthy because I forgave you. It means I don't hang on to resentment and bitterness, but it doesn't mean you've changed for the better. As long as you are relationally unhealthy, you will try to do things that'll hurt me.

The abuse could come from harsh words, slander, lying, backstabbing, etc., but as an illustration I'm going to use the example of physical violence.

"It looks like he bruised you up pretty bad."

"He did, but I forgave him for beating me."

"That's great! Get away from him."

"But, but, I forgave him."

"That's great. Get away from him. Get out of the house and don't go back home."

"But I forgave him."

"I'm glad you did, but you've got a twenty-year history here of him being abusive. Why don't you stay away until he shapes up?"

Just because you forgive someone, doesn't mean you allow yourself to be harmed over and over again.

Forgiveness is not a false sense of pardon where you say you've forgiven but really just count wrongs and wait for the opportune time to compound old wrongs onto any new wrongs. Who are we not to forgive, when we have been forgiven the greatest sin debt of all—if you know Jesus Christ as your Savior—and I'm talking about the debt that would cast us to Hell with no hope for eternity.

Imagine my spouse had a bad day and I said something innocent that absolutely set her off and sent her into a tirade where she demoralized almost every area of my manhood and my providership. My response to that pain would cause me to withdraw from her and act indifferent and uncaring. But the Lord emphasizes forgiveness, so let's imagine how His Holy Spirit would converse with me.

"All right, Rick. Your wife said some pretty nasty things to you, and I know they were hurtful and wrong. But why do you act so negatively toward her now? You realize the way you're acting is sin. It's your way of getting back at her, acting out in unforgiveness. You can act that way if you wish. But who you are to act that way when I forgave you of your sin debt?"

"I know, Lord. But you don't realize how bad she hurt me."

"Yes I do, and I'm sensitive to the fact she hurt you fairly bad when she said those things. But you're choosing not to forgive her? Didn't I forgive your sins and pardon you from Hell? Explain how you can't forgive for something small like that when I've saved you from an eternity of condemnation."

"I can't, Lord."

"Then why don't you give me your rights and let me deal with it my way?"

"But I want to do it. You see, I can do it better than you can. I want her to hurt."

"No, that's not the objective. What we want her to do is change, not hurt. Your flesh wants her to hurt because you want to get back. I want her to change so she is transformed more into my likeness and so you two will have a greater sense of Us-ness."

Your anger, your bitterness, and your resentment are the stones you throw. The Pharisees had real stones, but your words and your attitudes are modern stones to throw, and they hurt, too.

Unforgiveness at its deepest level

When you think back to the Pharisees carrying the stones they were going to use to stone the woman, have you ever wondered how many stones you actually carry around in your heart? How many stones would you say you carry? One? Two? Ten? Some want to say zero, but I imagine there are few who could say that. How about one hundred and seventy of them? Whoa, that's a lot.

Now how much do you think each stone weighs? Let's say each stone we carry weighs about a pound. So if you're carrying around five stones, you're carrying an extra five pounds around with you. If you were carrying one hundred stones, you're dragging around an extra one hundred pounds around with you wherever you go. That's a lot of resentment, bitterness, pain, anger, and whatever other harmful emotions. And you just can't drop them off and leave them in the closet. They go with you wherever you go. If you desire the right to be mad and not forgive, you have the weight to carry around with you as well.

"That's fine," the Lord might say. "If you want your rights, go ahead and keep them. Oh, by the way, if you would give up your rights, I would also remove the weights from you. But I respect your right for vengeance because I know what they did. If you want to keep your rights, you can also keep the weight."

Jesus invited, "Come to me, all of you who are weary and carry heavy burdens, and I will give you rest" (Matthew 11:28). What is that heaviness?

It's not extra weight around your midriff because you need to watch what you eat. It has to do with the heaviness of the human heart. The emotional stones—including fear and shame—we carry around is the heaviness Jesus was referring to. He took all the struggles, loneliness, and heartaches from us, and exchanged them with peace which passes all understanding. When we give up our vendetta rights to the Lord, we also release the heaviness that weighs us down and keeps us from enjoying life. The Lord wants to take those weights from us because we weren't created for that level of pain.

If I choose to stay resentful and carry that weight around, who suffers? I do. I will be the person who suffers. If married, your us-ness—your sense of connectedness—will suffer also. It's very hard to have us-ness and hang onto resentment, bitterness, and anger. When you decide to throw the stone, you may think you're getting what you want. You may say the one phrase that hurts the other person so bad that they're put in their place and you'll even feel good for doing it in your anger, and your flesh will make sure you feel good about it. Don't fool yourself. You're not just harming them; you're harming yourself because you're breaking your relationship with your Father. So this is dangerous, because wrapped up in your stones is unforgiveness. If I give up my rights I give up the weight. Why would I want to hang onto the rights if I know they're hurting me? One reason is to have a feeling of control. Another could be revenge. Why do you want revenge, and why do you want control? There is a certain selfish motivation underneath it all.

For years, I hadn't forgiven my stepmother for what I perceived as her harsh, distant attitude towards us kids. She was the only mother I'd known since I was three, and for years I wouldn't forgive her and would lash out at her verbally, but I could never pull myself away from her. Did you know unforgiveness binds you emotionally to your offender? As long as you don't forgive, you're not free; you are bound to them. Thirty years could elapse and when you think of this hurtful individual you still struggle with the emotions.

As I was struggling through this issue with my stepmother I sensed the Lord ask, "What do you want from her?"

"I want her to be my mother," I replied. I just wasn't ready to give up my stones. After some mental inspection, I surmised it was because I wanted something from her. I wanted to be right. I wanted to hear "I'm sorry. I was wrong." Then I'd get to say, "You bet you were." One time after berating her, I finally got to hear those words; I forced an apology out of her. But after it was all said and done, I didn't accept it. Although I got what I wanted, I couldn't accept them because they weren't given freely. It is godly sorrow which produces repentance (2 Corinthians 7:10). There was no real sorrow. I just beat her down with my words. What did I really want? I just wanted her to be my mother. Some of you might be in the same situation. You want that person to admit they're wrong and to admit they're a louse as a friend or a mate. That's why you hang onto those stones. You want to beat them with it until you get what you want. When they finally admit they're lousy, terrible, wrong, and they're the problem with the relationship, you'll get what you think you wanted because you're the one in control. Here's the problem with that. First, the stones you threw, even though you had the right, were from sin. In Ephesians 4:26, the Bible says, "Be angry, but don't sin." So now that you've got your momentary pleasure by appeasing your flesh, you will have to deal with a new feeling—condemnation. Your enemy, Satan is sure to pounce on you mercilessly. And you're just as wrong in God's eyes when you strike out at your offender for the wrong they've done to you. Your relationships can never be healthy that way because you both are beating each other. When you're wounded and hurt, how can you give to anyone if you're trying to heal yourself? The only real healing will come when you're obeying the Father. He designed relationships to work a certain way, and He's set boundaries and rules to make them work efficiently.

What does a good apology look like?

Did you know nowhere in the scripture does it tell us to say, "I'm sorry?" Nowhere in the Bible is there a command to apologize. In fact the Word of God never tells us to apologize. Did you know an apology is not a confession of wrong doing?

There are little ways you hurt others. You may say, "Okay, so when I ignored her, she got hurt. She just needs to get over it." Do you care that you hurt her? Obviously not. If you did, you'd be more sympathetic. How would you feel if she said the same thing to you?

Sometimes we'll try to minimize the damage. You'll say, "Well, it wasn't my intent to hurt her." It still begs the question—do you care? If you don't, drop any expectations of your friendship or your marriage getting close and intimate.

"Yeah, but it wasn't my intent to hurt her."

It doesn't matter whether it was your intent or not if you refuse to express sorrow for the hurt you've caused. Let's look at this example. You and I are good friends, and we're just sitting and talking while I'm cleaning my gun. As I'm cleaning, my weapon accidently fires and shoots you. Suddenly you're lying on the floor with a bullet hole in your side.

"You shot me!"

"Hey!" I reply. "I didn't mean to."

Do you really think I care that I shot him? No, I'm busy defending my position of 'innocence.' Isn't it strange how our pride and selfishness can get in the way and blind us from the fact that we're bleeding our relationships emotionally, when we hurt our others emotionally, and say, "Hey, why don't you just get over it?" You might not have been motivated to hurt them, but you still caused the pain. Just because you didn't mean to cause pain, doesn't mean you didn't cause it. The all-important question is, "do you care." If you do, it will motivate you to ease the pain for the one you unintentionally hurt.

One day I hurt my wife over something and I didn't realize what I did, but it caused her pain and made her feel unloved. Did I tell her to get over it? No. I love my wife and I don't want her to feel unloved. I want her to feel loved and connected. I want that Us-ness there. So when she confided in me and told me what I'd done, I listened. Yes, I could feel the emotional part of my brain and my flesh getting defensive, but I stepped back from that, listened, and said, "You know, I don't want you to feel unloved, and it saddens me that I hurt you. Will you forgive me? I would never want to hurt you, honey." She forgave me. If you notice, I didn't apologize. Apologies would not make me responsible for my wrong, admitting my wrong would. And it would not give her the opportunity to decide what she'd do with her feelings now that she knows I know what I did was wrong.

Godly sorrow produces repentance. Repentance means there's been a change of behavior or attitude. Worldly sorrow leads to death, the Bible says. Not just physical death, but it leads to death of a relationship, death of a marriage, death of a friendship, death of a parent/child relationship. It leads to death because worldly sorrow isn't concerned about the people that you hurt. Who is it concerned with? Just me.

If we're going to do true forgiveness, saying "I'm sorry" isn't going to suffice. We must do what the Bible teaches, which is confess and forgive. When I've been hurt by someone, I need to forgive them. When I've hurt someone, there needs to be godly sorrow in my heart that will motivate me to confession. When I confess what I've done wrong to the one who I've wronged, it produces repentance in me, and I admit, "I did this. I was wrong. I don't want to hurt you. Can you forgive me?" Godly sorrow motivates the wronged to forgive.

I was doing a premarital session with a couple for a week, and I don't think the guy realized he had some habits that hurt his potential mate. I had them do the dialogue guide which helped them air their feelings, but I went a step farther with it so they could clarify some issues in their relationship. The young man listened to what his fiancée described as things painful to her. I was proud of him. Without coercion, he realized, "Wow! I have disappointed you. I have hurt you." It wasn't his intent, but he saw what he was doing. Instead of thinking that she needed to get over it, his heart was saddened that he'd done and said some things that harmed her.

As I watched this transpiring, I asked, "I can sense you're hurting for her. What does that prompt you to do?"

"I need to tell her I was wrong and ask her to forgive me."

"That's a great place to go, but I don't need to be here. This is for you two alone," I said and left the premarital session for several moments so they could have their private time as the Lord was doing some work in their hearts.

Remember, nobody gets it right all the time. Forgiveness is something that needs to be practiced every day. I make mistakes, and I might hurt my wife, but I need to go to her for forgiveness. And when she hurts me, I must be ready to extend forgiveness to her. Dr. James McDonald, pastor of Harvest Bible Church in the Chicago area, said, "In any relationship, you need several big forgivenesses and a truckload of small forgivenesses."

Why the emphasis on forgiveness? None of us is perfect, and all of us mess up at one point or another. I will hurt somebody incidentally or accidently. I can be misunderstood which might cause hurt. I can also say the right thing at the wrong time to the wrong person. Many things can cause rifts in relationships. Forgiveness bridges the gaps.

So what does a good forgiveness confession look like? A good confession sounds like, "Forgive me. I was wrong. And not only was I wrong, I realize now what I did. I hurt you."

Forgiveness and healing

We all mess up, we all make mistakes, and we all sin. We make decisions and say words that harm people we love and, sometimes, to people we don't like. Once done, those things can't be undone.

We sin against the Lord by conducting ourselves wickedly, immorally, or sinfully. Once we've sinned it can't be reversed. We're guilty. The Lord knew that with guilt comes the heavy weight of condemnation and shame. The Lord cared enough for us to give us an escape plan. In 1 John 1:9, the Bible says, "If you confess your sins, [Jesus] is faithful and just to forgive you of your sins and cleanse you of all unrighteousness."

If you have the right motive behind seeking the Lord's forgiveness for sin, what would be the main motivation to obey the scripture? *Because God said to?* No, that's not motivation. *Because it frees me from the bondage of guilt and shame?* It does do that, but that's not the motivation.

Isaiah 53:5 says, "[Christ] was wounded for our transgressions and He was bruised for our iniquities."

Do you care that Jesus willingly suffered and died on the cross so you wouldn't have to be totally separated from Him and everyone else in a place called Hell? Does it sadden your heart at all when think He who did nothing wrong was afflicted with the penalty for your sin? When you were cold and insensitive, when you were sarcastic and hateful, He took a nail for that. Are you moved at all by the fact He endured the full wrath of God so it wouldn't fall on you? If that's the case, it should produce a sense of remorse since you know the sin you've committed added to His suffering.

"Lord, I had a bad attitude with my wife tonight at the restaurant. I know you died for that sin for me, but I don't want to hurt you because I love you." From that godly sorrow, I'll be prompted to do something else. "Lord, would you forgive me for my stinking attitude? I am so thankful for your promise that if I confess my sins that you're faithful and just to forgive me and cleanse me of all unrighteousness. Lord, it breaks my heart that I keep hurting you."

The Lord instantly forgives you and places you back into a right relationship with Him. This produces a sense of gratefulness which, in PET scans, actually shows energy changes in the brain between the forgiving and unforgiving people.

When I'm back in a right relationship with the Lord, I can sense Him saying, "You know I hold nothing against you, and your sin is a dead issue to me because the blood of Christ has cleansed you. However, you didn't just sin against me. Who else did you hurt?"

"My wife."

"Now read James 5:16, go to your wife, and obey what my scripture commands you to do."

I went and looked it up. *Confess your sins to each other and pray for each other so that you may be healed.*

What was my motivation to go and confess my wrongdoing to her? It saddened my heart that I hurt her. Why? Because I love her. If she's practicing the biblical commands, she will freely extend forgiveness because she's already freely received forgiveness from Christ. So the pattern is she forgives me, we restore the Us-ness in the relationship, and I commit not to sin against her again. I realize when I do those things that hurt her and I stop doing them because I don't want to hurt her. It becomes a self-checking mechanism. I'm motivated to become a better person. If you keep asking, "Will you forgive me?" but keep doing those things that hurt, I would argue that you're not truly repentant. True forgiveness drives you to want to become a better person. And because you want to be a better person for the Lord and for others, you'll change what you do.

Here's something important you need to remember. Just because a person chooses to forgive you, doesn't mean they're not hurting. Sometimes, we ask for forgiveness and assume they should just get over it. It doesn't work that way. That's why we must practice all of what James 5:16 states, "Confess your sins one to another and then it says and pray for each other that you may be healed." Just because I forgive, doesn't mean there is healing. If a Christian brother plows over me with his SUV, and I get put in the hospital, I can forgive him. Will I still have the effects of that event? Of course, I do; there must be a healing process that takes place before I can leave the hospital.

When I hurt my friend and ask her and the Lord to forgive me, then I pray the Lord would bring healing to her heart and I pray for the healing of our relationship. It's important to practice all of what that scripture dictates. That's why a lot of relationships don't heal. Even though there's forgiveness, there's not a lot of healing that takes place. You have to earn trust back. Just because you forgive someone doesn't mean you trust them. However, if I have godly sorrow, and I'm praying for your healing and trying to not hurt you in that way again because I want you to heal, the trust level is going to grow because I'm purposefully trying to rebuild it.

Every step of forgiveness is crucial for the survival and the thriving of the relationship. None of us are perfect, and we need to extend forgiveness to others as much as we need it ourselves.

* 9 *

UNDERSTANDING THEIR LANGUAGE

We hear people speak to us everyday. We speak to people everyday, whether it is face-to-face, via cell phone, e-mail, or text messaging. We speak, but does real communication occur? To speak is simply putting together consonant and vowels sounds into a comprehensible sentence. Just because somebody is talking to you doesn't necessarily mean I know what they're talking about. Someone could have a highly intelligent conversation with me, but if he's speaking in French, I won't understand him. Unfortunately, two people speaking the same language may not understand what the other person is saying either.

Often the speaker knows exactly what he's thinking but might not clearly communicate or may be misunderstood by the listener. On the other hand, the listener may have a predetermined idea that could distort his understanding of what the speaker is really saying. Understanding in communication is vital to have a prosperous, successful, and enjoyable relationship with anyone.

For example, I (Johnny) once went in to my hair designer to get my hair shaped nicely before a presentation.

"Just give me a trim," I said, thinking she'd know I only meant to clip the ends.

As she cut, I saw much more hair than I wanted coming off. "You're not cutting it too short, are you?" I asked.

"No. I'm doing exactly what you asked," she responded.

By the time the process had finished, a lot more hair was on the floor than I'd anticipated.

The next time I needed my hair "trimmed," I asked her, "What do you think I mean when I say I'd like a trim?"

"A trim is at least one inch. If you only want your ends shaped, tell me you want this," she said, and held up her index finger and thumb pressed together.

This may be a simple example but it shows how easily people can be speaking and hearing, but how there was no understanding.

Do you know that 80% of the problems in relationships don't need to be solved? They only need to be understood. We try to move into the solution mode too quickly. Two people, or two parties, can disagree, but when you understand each other you can move on to more productive steps.

So what are some of the key elements of understanding? First, there must be a speaker. Second, there must be a listener. These two will switch roles throughout the conversation in order to establish a clear path of understanding. It's like building a brick pathway one stone at a time. One speaks, laying down his brick in the pathway. Another listens, putting his into place. It's the third stone that's very important. Here's where the listener paraphrases what the speaker says to assure that he understands what the speaker is saying. If you say what you think the speaker means and the speaker agrees, you can proceed to build the path of communication. But if what you paraphrase is not what the speaker means, the speaker can restate or clarify what he was saying, thus the two of you avoid a misunderstanding which could have stopped your path-building process after only two bricks. It's not important whether or not you agree; the key is to show you understand. There are basic rules for both the speaker and the listener to produce understanding.

First, determine who the speaker is. This seems fairly simple to figure out, right? Well, maybe not. Unfortunately, in many conversations we don't have a speaker and a listener. We have two speakers. While one speaks, the other's formulating a comeback and interrupts at strategic moments. Neither tries to understand; both just try to get their point across.

The Bible gives us excellent wisdom concerning communication and understanding. "…be quick to listen, slow to speak, and slow to get angry" (James 1:19).

A pastor once said, "Since we have two ears and only one mouth, we should listen twice as much as we talk." Superb advice. The key to any conversation is the ability to actually hear the message the other person's trying to convey. Instead of focusing on what you think and wanting to just get it out there, when you listen to what someone is saying you are hearing what's in another's heart. How priceless it is for someone to share that with you. But when you blurt out stuff and blab away, you miss out on the treasure someone's about to share with you. When you hear what someone shares with you, you gain understanding. Understanding is the lifeblood of any relationship.

That's why we should be quick to listen, slow to speak, and slow to get angry. Think about it. Does the Lord interrupt you when you're yelling at Him? Of course not. He listens and seeks to understand where you're coming from. Does He agree with you all the time? No, but what He doesn't do is bring up past history. "Wait a moment. I remember the time I did this for you. And what about the times you failed and forsook me?" The Lord doesn't do that to us. We shouldn't do it to each other. When in a disagreement the issue isn't to solve it. You just talk about it and build a bridge of understanding.

The skill of determining "the speaker" and "the listener" is powerfully successful although it feels artificial. If you train yourself to use those skills, you'll reap fantastic benefits. In marriage, you actually counteract all the danger signs that predict distress and divorce. Why? Because if I am speaking and my spouse is listening, it takes away the defense mechanism of withdrawing or avoiding. It forces us to do the hard work of communicating even when we don't want to.

In Chapter 14, I'll elaborate on a technique called **Speak The Truth In Love.** In this communication skill, there are thirteen sentence stems that can be used to civilly discuss any issues. By using this technique, the relationship gears stays engaged and you'll be cruising again before long instead of grinding. By one person listening while the other is talking, anger escalation is snuffed out. If you practice hearing and understanding what the other is sharing, how could you blow your top? This skill eliminates the invalidation or negative interpretations common in verbal clashes.

By adhering to these skills, you actually counteract 90% of the danger signs that predict distress in relationships and divorce in marriages. When you determine the speaker-listener format you communicate well when needed, and as you practice it, you learn to communicate better even if you don't use the full structure. Excellent communicators are worth their weight in gold in businesses, friendships, sports, and, most importantly, in families.

I learned these skills and was practicing them nearly a decade before my wife began initiating them. Today it works well in our marriage just as it does in my other relationships. When I use these with co-workers, the communication never escalates, even if we don't agree. As long as I stuck with the structure, even if they didn't, animosity can't grow because there's no feedback route. If I do it with my kids, there is no feedback. I am not becoming part of a potential problem. We understand each other first. We come up with a resolution later. That's just how I communicate, and it's effective.

If you approached me to share something with me, I automatically consider you the speaker. Afterward, I repeat what I think you meant; I don't repeat what I heard you say. "So what you're saying is this," or "What you're saying is that. Oh, okay. I understand. May I share my views now?" In my mind, you're giving me the opportunity to speak.

If you start invalidating me or what I say, it would be obvious you don't know the skills. "Hey, wait a minute," I say. "I am not asking you to agree with me. Just hear me out." I lovingly push you into the role of a listener. This produces a sense of safety where we both can share our views. Using these skills will affect every part of every relationship you've got.

Two more vital ingredients for the most vital of relationships

The most challenging but most rewarding and blessed relationship most will ever experience is marriage. Communication and understanding are foundational to success in marriage. But what are the keys that unlock intimacy? Emotional openness and physical closeness. Before we delve into that we've got to look at what keeps people from reaching this stage. Few seem intimate in their relationships nowadays. So we must explore how we've gone wrong before we can enjoy how we can do things right. When a couple will not share their deep feelings and will retract from nearness, research shows that the danger signs or predictors for divorce and distress are in that relationship. These predictors are the cancer of spousal relationships: avoidance and withdrawal. What precipitates these signs? Anger and the failure to deal with it.

Ephesians 4:25-27 says, "So put away all falsehood and speak truth with your neighbor because we all belong to each other. And don't sin by letting anger gain control over you. Don't let the sun go down while you are still angry, for anger gives a mighty foothold to the Devil."

Is it okay to be angry? Yes, even the scripture says it, but the warning is "don't let anger gain control of you." It's one of the few emotions that you actually see in scripture. The healthiest emotions we can experience are on opposite ends of the spectrum. In the Epistle to the Philippians, we are continually exhorted to be joyful. Christ Jesus was more joyful than anyone, even though He knew He'd have to bear the wrath of God for the sins of the world. But Christ also displayed anger. His anger was holy and justified; ours may or may not be. The Bible gives allowance for anger; it's an outlet for frustration and pain. But if that anger is bottled up and stored it ferments into an acid that not only destroys relationships around you and erodes your relationship with God, but it begins to eat you alive. And that's when the devil steps in. Unsettled anger relinquishes territory in your spiritual life where Satan can fly his corrupt flag. Not dealing with your anger produces resentment and bitterness and spiritually it looks like a wide open door for Satan to walk in to wreak havoc in your life and your relationship.

Do you want to know why marriages are failing in Christian homes? It's because the devil has a foothold in their heart and into their relationship because they don't deal with anger. Forgiveness is the remedy for relinquishing anger, and we'll go over that in detail later.

Unresolved anger puts distance between you and your spouse. It places distance between you and the Lord. This is when you begin to see avoidance and withdrawal. Twenty years of research shows that about 70% of the time, it's the men who withdraw. What does withdrawal look like? The individual will close up, turn and say, "I can't deal with this," then walk away.

Another may look like this: "Do we have to talk about this again?"

Not all relationships have the males withdrawing first, but in that type of atmosphere there are going to be a typical avoidance-withdrawal pattern. Gender differences are what we must understand in this dynamic. Men have a tendency to withdraw; women tend to pursue. If a guy is withdrawn, it's because subconsciously and relationally, he fears some sense of conflict. He's apprehensive about the conflict getting out of hand thus he doesn't want to deal with it and withdraws. What will the woman do? Pursue. It could be called nagging, complaining, or intruding, but she is trying to resolve the problem. This pursuer/withdrawal pattern is circular, and can create a downward spiral because neither understands what the other's doing. As he withdraws, she pursues and thinks, *Well, I'm not connected with this guy. I need to connect with him because we need to talk this out.* That's her reasoning, even if her words or actions don't come across as concerned or loving.

Escalation is when, at some point, there's nowhere farther you can withdrawal since she keeps pursuing. At that point you stand your ground and start what you were trying to avoid—getting into the fight mode. Once you're back into the fight, even though you fear the conflict, anger's vented. You may hear yourself say things like, "Well, there you go again." Your voice raises, and you start doing exaggerated movements you weren't doing earlier. No longer are you avoiding the fight, you're escalating it. It's now winner take all. No prisoners.

Proverbs 29:11 says, "A fool gives full vent to anger, but the wise quietly hold it back." Wise people don't give in to their anger. They're able to control it instead of allowing it to control them. This is a sign of maturity.

Proverbs 12:18 says, "Reckless words pierce like a sword, but the tongue of the wise brings healing." When you are angry, are thinking about what you're saying? Oh no. You say things in your anger that you "don't mean." Dr. Herb Reavis, Jr. of North Jacksonville Baptist Church said, "When you're squeezed, whatever's in you is what comes out." The Lord Jesus Christ said, "Out of the abundance of the heart, the mouth speaks" (Matthew 12:34). I, too, argue that whatever is in your heart will come out of your mouth. We never say things we "don't mean." We might say things we actually do mean, but didn't intend to say out loud.

Some people say, "Sticks and stones may break my bones but words will never hurt me." Is that true? The Bible says, "Life and death are in the power of the tongue" (Proverbs 18:21). If you call someone "stupid" long enough, that person will believe it. If you tell someone they're incompetent, dumb, fat, and ugly, they will assimilate those words and begin to live that way. As things begin to escalate, you start invalidating your partner, putting down your mate, and making sarcastic comments to tear the other person down. Outside of your relationship with Christ, the most precious thing you own is your value and sense of worth.

When you begin tearing down another's value and worth, you are undermining that relationship. Sooner or later, that person's going to say, "That's enough." Among friends and in marriages when you try to invalidate the other person and what they've accomplished, a fight becomes inevitable. You'll begin to attack and insult each other. Of course, these actions force you onto the path of negative interpretation where no matter what's said it'll be considered a stab. Any semblance of rational thinking and listening has ceased because anger has full control, not you. In this stage, I might say something to my wife that I didn't mean in a negative way, but because she's not listening well and all of this angry energy is coursing through her body, she interprets something innocuous I said as harmful.

In my defense, I say, "That's not what I meant."

"Well, that's what you said!" she'll retort.

"That's not what I meant."

Do you hear the escalation?

We aren't listening to each other. There's no real communication going on now. Because there's no understanding things, I didn't mean to be harmful are now interpreted in a negative way. Unchecked, this pattern will create relational devastation long term.

People with new relationships may have already developed this pattern, and you might say, "It doesn't destroy us."

That's great. But let's take an engaged couple for example. While courting, you're willing to put up with anything. She'll say to herself, "Oh, he's a wonderful guy. He's so self-assured, forceful, and speaks his opinion. I love that about him. We may trade insults every now and then, but we're just playing."

Five years later…

"You're so opinionated, you imbecile. Why won't you ever listen to me? And why are you always cutting me down? If I'd known you'd be so mean I wouldn't have married you."

Had either changed? No, but her willingness to tolerate has. Before initiating vital relationships, we need to look ahead to predict how today's attitudes and words will affect tomorrow. Negative and hateful words will erode any positives in the relationship, the fun, the friendship, the dreams, and the hopes.

To avoid all this heartache, the dynamics of communication must be learned so you can negate the predictors of distress and divorce while building a firm foundation. If you want successful communication with intimacy, you must practice emotional openness and physical closeness. Emotional openness means I'm being candid with you, willing to be vulnerable, and willing to take a risk. It means taking all the armor off and exposing my soul to you. You're offering unconditional trust. You're not giving to your partner what you want, but what they need. Physical closeness is simply being in near proximity—not yelling from the room next door or down the hall.

An elderly couple was once asked, "How have you two kept your marriage together and successful for so long?"

The old man said, "We never fight or argue unless we are holding hands."

It's hard to destroy each other emotionally when you're in a loving position physically.

* 10 *

GUARD YOUR HEART

Above all else, guard your heart, for it affects everything you do.

We read this in the Proverbs 4:23. Guard your heart from wrong motives, from distorted thinking, and from suspicious lies. We are also to stay vigilant against people and actions that would harm us emotionally. When we guard our hearts, we protect ourselves from the deceit causing confusion and frustration in relationships. Guarding our hearts doesn't mean we isolate ourselves and keep everybody at a distance in order not to be tricked and hurt. We guard our hearts to protect the vital relationships around us so they can flourish.

It's interesting in the church today how we talk a lot about knowing God's Word, memorizing God's Word, and hiding it in our hearts, but, respectfully, I think we've forgotten what that means. In some ways, we've lost the idea that the Word of God was not just meant for the rational mind. It was meant to be experienced in the human heart.

In your personal relationship with the Lord, even Jesus said, "Love the Lord your God with all your heart, all your soul, and all your mind" (Matthew 22:37).

We use the word heart often, but we don't really understand it in spiritual context. You aren't supposed to have the Word of God strictly in your mind. You should also have it in your hearts. What does that mean? Your heart is actually the essence of your complete soul: mind, will, and emotions.

- If someone is cold-hearted, what does that mean? Unfeeling. Indifferent. Uninterested. Cynical. Calculating.
- What do you see if someone's broken-hearted? Distraught. Crestfallen. Hurting.
- If someone's heartless, how would you describe them? Merciless. Mean. Unsympathetic.
- How would you depict a warm-hearted person? Friendly. Amicable. Winsome.

What's so interesting is even though you can't physically look at someone's "heart," you can sense it in their inflections, tones, and body language. Someone might tell you, "Well yah, I love you," and yet they act cold, indifferent and unfeeling, and when you're hurting they don't care. He'll tell you from his mind he cares, but you can sense his heart. You can sense whether a person is cold and indifferent or if they are loving, warm, and caring.

You may be dating someone who says one thing, but their heart suggests another. You might want to believe what she says, but you intuitively sense her heart speaks the opposite. Sometimes you better hold onto what you sense; there may be some evidence of truth.

The Bible tells us to guard our hearts. Why? How do you experience life? Is it just by examining it with your intellectual mind? Let's say you're standing on the foothills of the Rocky Mountains. You look across the panorama of majestic, jagged peaks towering over you and reaching to the sky. All around the base of the mountains are armies of evergreens. Snow like white frosting clings in the clefts and crevices of the rocks. And behind it all, the sun takes its slow journey to sleep behind the rocky giants leaving a kiss of pink and orange in the darkening heavens. Now do you take this all in and think, *those are America's youngest mountain ranges, and the reason they're there is because a long time ago formations of...*No. You stand their awed and experience this breathtaking view. You know intellectually it's there because your eyes have seen it, but there's an emotional side that's encompassing this whole thing as well.

Guard your heart because it's there that we understand where our relationships are and where they're not. You'll know if a person's heart is in the relationship and you'll also know if it isn't.

Commitments

Guarding your heart in a healthy way requires making commitments to the relationships you're involved in. There are two types: commitment by devotion and commitment by constraint.

Commitment by devotion

Devotion implies intrinsic motivation. This is the idea that I'm in this relationship because I want to be here and I'm devoted to you because I love you. The signs of commitment by devotion are clear. There is a strong affection toward your mate. It has a strong sense of, "I'm in this relationship for the long haul. I see us together 40 years from now."

There was a large study done in the 1980's of older couples married 45 years and above compared to those of younger couples. One significant difference between the groups was those married 45 years all said the when they got married they couldn't perceive themselves in the future without their mate, while the younger could. In the longevity group, there was a sense of going the distance. As a matter of fact, interesting research done at the University of Denver shows that couples who have a long-term relational idea actually purchase long-term appliances. Couples without a sense of commitment don't tend to do this. The depth of a couple's commitment even affects their buying practices.

Commitment by constraint

This commitment is not rooted in devotion but obligation. In other words, "I'm committed to this relationship because of the kids." Or you might think, "I'm here because if we break this off, then I don't have the money to go on my own and you're the one who makes all the money."

Possibly in your mind you'll consider alterative monitoring, which is just a fancy way of saying, "Well, I've been in this marriage 20 years and gained a little weight. No one else would want me, so I'll just stay here because at least I've got somebody that's going to want me, even though you don't want me that much."

There are religious pressures. "God hates divorce, and so as much as I don't like being with you and as much as I don't like this relationship, I'm going to stay in it because of God.

There are also social pressures. Your society or your social group may be against marriage failing. Parents might be against divorce, so you stay in the relationship, because you don't want to disappoint them.

Some stay in the relationship because they don't want to go through the hassles of divorce. Compared to any unhappiness, the costs to terminate are too great.

If you want a healthy relationship and if you want to protect it, there may be times when there's commitment by constraint, and this is not negative. If, because of conflict, I don't feel like being married anymore, but you don't allow yourself to leave because of the kids, that's not a bad thing. Hopefully, the obligations keep you there, and get you focused and committed on the relationship so you can develop some devotion again. Devotion won't just happen. It takes hard work. Communication and understanding will be vital, but it definitely will be rewarding. As you see, obligation is not strictly negative; you just don't want this to be your only reason for staying long term.

A loss of affection means your relationship is no longer guarded. It becomes a reservoir for pain and hurt. Where your marriage started out with two-becoming-one in an atmosphere of intimacy, it devolves into just two people living as roommates. You've lost a sense of Us-ness. "What is that?" you may ask. Let me remind you, Us-ness is the most important ingredient in the intimacy recipe. 'Us-ness' is the unity that is built between two people that leads to selflessness and intimacy, and you'll hear it referred often because 'Us-ness' is vital to relationships. I'll develop the uniqueness and the importance of it throughout the book.

Why the negative?

If there's no Us-ness, you'll drift apart until you finally separate emotionally, physically, and relationally.

"Why are you emphasizing that negative stuff?"

If you don't protect your marriage, it'll be shredded. More likely than at any other time, you are more likely to divorce right now in America in the first three years, even if you're a Christian. Unfortunately, many are sitting around with an unhealthy relationship, but they're in denial because of the effort it'll take to deal with it. So let's not be foolish. I am a realist, not an idealist. I deal with reality and then go from there. If you know the truth, you'll be made free. Deny the truth and you'll be enslaved to bad habits and destructive relationships. And so if you're going to protect your relationship, I want you to understand the negative process you'll need to avoid, and then the principles you'll need to initiate in your relationship to enjoy it and make it prosper. Often times, the best offense is a good defense. So we're going to look at the opposition to having a great relationship.

Be cautious about the phases in this downward spiral in your own marriage.

- Phase1—The disillusionment stage
- Phase 2—The hurt stage
- Phase 3—The anger stage
- Phase 4—Ambivalence
- Phase 5—The disaffection stage

These are self-explanatory, so I'll spend only a short amount of time displaying them.

Phase 1—The disillusionment stage

When there are feelings of disappointment and disenchantment with the marriage, you've reached this unhealthy destination. You begin thinking something like, *I can't believe I did this. Why did I even decide to marry this person? How was I supposed to know my mate was going to turn out like this?*

Some people will come into counseling and say, "Well, Dr. Marks, I didn't know. I could've never guessed things would turn sour the way they have."

"That's not true," I'll say. "You did see the signs. Didn't he outright lie to you before you got married?"

"Yea."

"Didn't he lie to your folks right in your presence? Didn't you know he couldn't be trusted?"

"Yea."

"Well then, you saw the signs. You knew it. You just chose not to accept it for what it was. You had to redefine what you saw so you'd see what you wanted."

Your thoughts at this stage bring an awareness that the relationship isn't going as well as expected. You have doubts about your partner or your decision to marry this person.

These are the behaviors that result: attempts to change yourself. You try harder to please your partner. You try to love harder, or be more attractive—or whatever you think will get them to notice you—to get them more involved in the relationship. Because you feel the relationship is one-sided, a sense of disillusionment begins. If you don't bring resolution in this phase, you move into the hurt stage.

Phase 2—The hurt stage

There's no clear-cut time frame on when you go from one stage to the next. It depends on how long you want to live in denial and keep trying to change yourself without your mate changing. When you realize your mate's on cruise-control while you're putting in all the effort, your thinking moves from disillusionment to hurt. Deep down you want them to care and sacrifice as much as you do. I see this so many times.

"Well, I tried for 15 years to be everything that he wanted me to be."

"Did it work?"

"No."

"Do you know why? It's because you were trying to change him. You can't change him. He doesn't want to change." Accept the reality and then you can make better decisions for the relationship that won't bury you under an impossible load.

In the hurt stage, you feel like you're treated unfairly, you're abused or you're alone. Abuse here can be loosely defined as emotional, mental, physical, or spiritual. Abuse isn't necessarily physical or sexual. You feel like your partner doesn't understand you. A mental balance sheet of rewards and costs of the relationship is mentally kept. You keep count of what he does or doesn't do, rewarding good and negative scores. At this point you're hurt, but you still try to justify the relationship. Behind it all, there's an awareness your emotional and social needs aren't being met, and you're thinking you're not important in your partner's life.

The behavior that results is that you start sharing with other people your personal problems. At this point, you start talking with friends, family, neighbors, or anybody about the marriage discrepancies.

Here's a wise consideration: If you want to protect your marriage, but you've got to talk, keep the information to a very small group of people. Share only with people you can confide in, who know you, and love you. If hurt gets too bad, then you go see a counselor, but don't go telling everybody. Don't go telling your Sunday school class, because that's a form of gossip. "I just gotta share something about my husband. Ya'll pray for him. He beats me." Tell somebody who can help you, not in a public format. It's disrespectful to him, and those kinds of men have very low self-images anyway. It's appropriate to confide, but be careful. Some people confide too much. Spreading the hurt to a broader audience intensifies the hurt and leads to the anger stage.

Phase 3—The anger stage

This is when resentment, hostility, indignation, and bitterness arise. You develop a keen awareness of accumulated hurts over time. Paramount in your thoughts is what you perceive to be your partner's wrong behaviors, and all blame is directed that direction. Negative thoughts of your partner begin to outweigh positive thoughts. You decrease trust in your partner's actions and motives.

At this stage, your behaviors center around expressing your emotions. You are no longer holding back how you feel. Hurt, anger, and disappointment is vocalized, and you confront your partner with grievances. You could begin to avoid your partner to protect yourself from further hurt, and sexual behavior diminishes into a duty or stops altogether. You have gone beyond "taking it to God in prayer, hoping and praying he will stop doing what he's doing."

You can't control what others do, but you can control what you do, and you do have the right to say, "No."

"You will not treat me that way."

"I will not be talked to in such a manner."

Definitely, bring your burdens and heartaches to the Lord, and He will comfort and guide you. But stand up for yourself as well. If you allow someone to hurt you or treat you disrespectfully, the bottom line is you can't change them. If you don't stand firm against abusive behavior, all that says is that you don't respect yourself. People who respect themselves don't allow others to habitually mistreat them.

If the anger isn't dealt with, you descend into the ambivalence stage.

Phase 4—The ambivalence stage

This is the relationally dangerous stage where start saying, "I don't care anymore." You alternate between the indecisive, unresolved thoughts of despair and hope concerning your partner and marriage. You're torn between trying to make the marriage work and wanting to give up. Here in America, ½ to 2/3 of all divorces are initiated by women. Research has defined this as the "walk-away wife syndrome." The reason women are walking away is because husbands aren't involved in the relationship. Ladies get tired of being neglected. What kills the relationship and causes them to give up and leave is the wife will spend many years talking about the neglect and the lack of involvement to no avail.

"Honey, this relationship is not healthy. There are problems here. We need to talk about it."

"Yea, yea. We'll do it later."

Time and again, the husband never does talk about it. To his delight, she eventually quits complaining. Do you know why? All her attempts to make the marriage work have been unfruitful. She now pours herself into her work, her kids, or whatever, but no longer into you. And then one day, she starts making what is called an Exit Strategy.

"I'm going to get a college degree, and once I get it, I'm out of here."

"I'm going to get a job and start my career."

The husband can't understand, after all this time, why she finally wants a career. She starts pocketing money into a secret account he didn't know about. She's formulating her Exit Strategy.

Finally, one day when you come home from work, she says, "We need to talk."

"What do you want to talk about this time?"

"We need to talk. I want a divorce."

This is where the husband's lack of discernment expresses itself. "You want a what?"

"I want a divorce."

"What? Wait a minute. What do you want a divorce for? I didn't know there was a problem. Why didn't you tell me?"

Once he says that is when the wife's rage pours out. "Tell you? Tell you? I've been telling you for 15 years and you haven't listened!"

There's a dramatic crossroad here. You've got his full attention now, and he realizes he's got to change. But you may have decided to end it. You've got your Exit Strategy in place, and you don't want to deal with it anymore. Michele Weiner-Davis in her book *Divorce-busting*, says, "if you stay in there, you have his attention. He will make efforts to change." Are you willing to wait a little longer to allow it to happen?

At this stage there is serious comparison between the reasons to stay and the costs to give up on the marriage. You evaluate the external forces of whether to stay or leave. Is it worth the money, the children, or God to keep me in this? All things begin to get weighed and people start their Exit Strategies during this phase. Initiating counseling or seeking trustworthy confidants is crucial to sort out your feelings.

Phase 5—The disaffection stage

You get detached, alienated, and apathetic. There's indifference toward your partner, and little desire to be emotionally close. You think your partner can't satisfy your needs, and any changes your partner makes are too late. Contact with your partner is avoided as much as possible. There is no desire for physical touching of any kind, and any communication is only small talk. You begin pursuing other interests and relationships outside of marriage. Can you hear how the marriage is dissolving itself?

Unless both people deal first with the spiritual problem, which is having a vibrant, pleasing relationship with Christ, and secondly, deal with their emotional baggage, they are going to hurt each other.

Love Deposits

Have you ever gone to the bank to withdraw money only to find out you've already spent it all? Love in marriage works the same way. If you make consistent deposits you build up a considerable savings account. When a withdrawal is taken out, it hardly phases the deposit that's already been made. Unfortunately, in the love category, too many of us have no deposits and we're living on credit, or love debt. By taking out love, and not replenishing your love bank account, you begin what I'm going to call love-busters.

The most wonderful emotion in the human experience is love. Without it, life's not worth living. You can live six weeks without food. You can live six days without water. But emotionally, you die in a matter of moments without love. As a rule, I need to deposit more love into my partner than I extract. I need to do more loving behaviors, more encouraging, more helping, and spend more time so when I do hurt my mate or do something boneheaded, there's a large abundance to draw from. If she's filled with love, she will think of my discrepancy as an exception instead of the norm.

Gary Smalley, in his book *Making Love Last Forever,* said that for every negative withdrawal we make it takes 10 deposits to make up for it. So we're not dealing with a 1 withdrawal—1 deposit scenario. Love must be deposited often to make up for the times I really mess up.

Love-busters

If you don't make a priority of protecting each other from your own selfish instincts and habits, you can become the greatest source of each other's unhappiness. Each of us has our own selfish instincts and habits, and you already know what they are. You may not want to accept them, but they're there. The reality is you'll take those selfish instincts and behavior habits and patterns into your relationship. It's your responsibility to control them to make the relationship better and less painful.

Remember, lack of empathy helps make thoughtlessness possible. Empathy is simply the ability to share another's emotions, thoughts, and feelings. If your mate is struggling or hurting, and you don't care, simply let her know it's not bothering you. I promise you that many love withdrawals will be sucked out of your account.

A selfish attitude is what we're trying to kill. Here's the wrong attitude:

"Well, you know what? This is just the way I am. You married me, and I'm simply being me. Deal with it."

How selfish.

Think of the greatest relationship of all: yours with the Lord. Could you use that excuse with Him?

"Hey, Lord it's the way I am. Can't you accept me the way I am?"

What do you think the Lord would say?

"I didn't make you to be helpless and powerless. I didn't save you to be controlled by your own selfishness. I made you to overcome. You can do all things through Christ who strengthens you. You choose not to. I have accepted you the way you are, but I don't want you to stay that way. I love you and empowered you when I came into you and birthed you spiritually to change. If you choose to remain immature, you create the consequences for your own choices."

We're going to look at five love-busters. Love-busters are repeated behaviors of one spouse that makes the other one unhappy. The premise here is to know what they are in order to avoid doing them.

Selfish Demands

Demands are nothing short of abuse forms. Manipulating, controlling, conniving, and lying are forms of demands used to get what you want. Thoughtful requests are a wise alternative to selfish demands. You choose to make selfish demands though, and if you do, you're being abusive.

You're thinking, "What are you talking about? I didn't hit her."

Physical abuse is not the only kind there is. You can emotionally abuse someone by berating them to the point they're not even sure what's right or wrong. You make them feel guilty when they're not even guilty by placing a weight on them to carry around because you didn't get what you wanted. Instead of demanding, respectfully explain to your spouse what you would like and allow your spouse the option of giving or denying. More times than not, your spouse won't know what you enjoy unless you inform them.

Don't expect them to be mind readers. Inform them lovingly instead of demanding. Your spouse's responses are so much more enjoyable when it's done out of love instead of coercion.

Disrespectful Judgments

This is where you attempt to straighten out your spouse's attitudes, beliefs, and behaviors by imposing your way of thinking through lectures, ridicule, threats, or other forceful means. If you want to protect your relationship, refrain from doing these. Use respectful persuasion, presenting your reasoning behind your position, and listen to your spouse with the willingness to admit that your spouse may be the one who's correct.

Angry Outbursts

When you become angry with your spouse, you threaten your spouse's safety and security in the relationship. You fail to provide for your spouse's protection when you deliberately attempt to hurt your spouse because of anger, using any form of verbal or physical abuse.

I know a lady who's been married for 29 years to a guy who likes that bizarre bondage stuff, and she thought she had to give into it. When she got pregnant with their first child, he was mad because the pregnancy got in the way of what he wanted to do sexually. He stayed mad at her and didn't talk to her for seven months, but it wasn't until their baby almost died that he started talking to her again. When she got pregnant the second and third time, he did the same thing. Since she expressed she wasn't interested in that weird, wacko bondage sex two years ago, he hasn't talked to her for that long. They live in the same house and sleep next to each other, but they don't talk. Some people get angry and hold it against you. It's not your problem. It's theirs. Resolution comes only when you use the communication skills and 'give each other the floor.'

Annoying Behavior

Annoying habits aren't things you try to do to bug your spouse. They're habits and activities that unintentionally cause your spouse to be unhappy. The way you eat, the way you clean or don't clean up after yourself, and discarding clothing on the floor and not picking them up are just some examples of annoying behaviors.

If you care enough about your partner, you'd take the effort to change those behaviors.

You could say, "This is the way I am!" That may be so, but those habits are still annoying. They are still bad habits.

One thing we must understand is that marriage will refine you. Marriage is designed to be a team effort and a joy. Unless you or your spouse change your habits and activities so that they make you both happy, instead of making only one of you happy, you'll eventually find you can't live with each other for long. Work hard to eliminate annoying habits.

Dishonesty

Simply put, dishonesty is failure to reveal to your spouse correct information about your emotions, reactions, personal history, daily activities, and plans for the future. Honesty is like a flu shot. It may give you a short, sharp pain, but it keeps you healthier over the following months.

Now with all that said, we want to deposit love into your spouse's emotional bank account, and by that I mean doing the things that it takes to keep the marriage healthy. Every person is different. Each spouse is different from one another, and so different things spell love to different individuals. I once heard someone say, "Just because your spouse isn't loving you the way you want doesn't mean they aren't loving you the best they can." I want to argue that point because of the extensive research that's been done. You can love your spouse the way they enjoy the best if you love them and do the research on them. What do I mean? Different things spell love for different people. An extensive resource on this matter is Gary Chapman's book *The Five Love Languages*. In his book we learn that there are five primary languages that speak love to people.

- Words of Affirmation
- Quality Time
- Receiving Gifts
- Acts of Service

- Physical Touch

The key is speaking their language, not showing them love in your language. The way we speak their language is by meeting their emotional needs. When each spouse invests time into understanding what spells love to the other, the marriage will blossom like never before.

* 11 *

SPEAK WELL AND LISTEN WELL

Communication is key in any relationship, whether it be work-related, sports, hanging out with your friend, talking to your children, or speaking to your wife. The foundation of effective communication is speaking well and listening attentively. Sound speech has no power if it isn't heard. In too many conversations, there are two people trying to express their ideas and feelings, but neither is heard, because they're both sharing but neither is listening. No relationship is easy; they all take hard work to maintain, but somehow we've gotten fooled into the idea that each partner in a relationship should know what is best for the other without communicating it. One of the bravest things you can do with someone is share your innermost thoughts and feelings with them. One of the greatest privileges you could ever experience is having someone tell you what's really going on in their mind and their emotions.

In marriage, the vital lifeblood of the union is the ability to speak and listen well. How often a good marriage dies because the couple who'd expressed that they loved each other can't work through their differences. Many differences that divide are small, and they wouldn't be an issue if one spouse would intelligently articulate while the other hushes, listens, and try to empathize with what the other is struggling with. Then of course, there must be reciprocation in the communication equation—the one who respectfully speaks must now respectfully listen to the one who'd been listening.

What I'm going to share with you in this chapter is a tool for effective communication. This is what I call "the **Speak Your Truth with Love** sharing guide." This guide is to help relationships weather conflict so there is little to no damage to the relationship. This active listening skill includes a Speaker (who completes each of the sentence stems below with respect and good will while practicing assertiveness) and a Listener (who paraphrases what he/she heard the Speaker share). **Important:** This is not a problem solving skill and the listener does not have to *agree* with the Speaker. Always ask permission before using this skill, and remember, when you want to talk might not be a good time for your partner. Be sure you agree on a good time to use the Speaker-Listener skills.

Below are the sentence stems to be used in the **Speak Your Truth with Love** sharing guide. I will list them, then explain through example how it works.

1. I see that you…(behavior)
2. When you do this I think it means…(your assumption)
3. Because of this, I feel…(your emotion)
4. I resent…
5. My fear about this is …
6. So, what I do as a reaction to this is…(your reactive behaviors)
7. What I would like you to do differently is…(specific request)
8. I think this will help our relationship by…
9. I realize that…
10. What I can do is…
11. I appreciate you for…
12. And I look forward to…
13. Thank you for listening.

This skill will not sound natural when you start to use it. It'll actually sound quite mechanical. The purpose is not to be articulate; it's to address problems in a non-confrontational manner so that the relationship won't grow cold, distant, and bitter. Your spouse can't read your mind, and your spouse can't know what your needs are and what actions and attitudes hurt you unless you reveal it.

I see that you…(behavior)
Speaker: I see that you won't give me five kisses a day.
Listener: You say I won't give you five kisses a day.

When you do this I think it means…(assumption)
Speaker: When you don't kiss me five times a day I think it means you really don't care about me or my needs.
Listener: You are saying I don't care about you or your needs if I don't kiss you five times a day.

Because of this I feel…(emotion)
Speaker: Because of this, I feel sad and I wonder if you really love me.
Listener: You feel sad and doubt whether I love you because I haven't kissed you five times a day.

I resent…
Speaker: I resent that you won't kiss me five times a day.
Listener: You resent that I haven't kissed you five times a day.

My fear about this is…
Speaker: My fear about this is that we'll slowly stop showing affection to each other and our marriage will grow cold and die.
Listener: You fear our relationship and our love for each other will wane if I don't kiss you five times a day.

So what I do as a reaction to this is…(your reactive behaviors)
Speaker: So what I do as a reaction to you not kissing me five times a day is I grow bitter, and I begin to worry about the health of our marriage.
Listener: You grow bitter and worried about our relationship if I don't kiss you five times a day.

What I would like you to do differently is…(specific request)
Speaker: What I would like you to do differently is plan out five specific

times during the day that you'll purposefully kiss me. That way you'll know how to meet my need and I'll have something to look forward to each day.

Listener: You would like me to plan out five times during the day that I will purposefully kiss you.

I think this will help the relationship by...

Speaker: I think this will help the relationship by you tangibly displaying your love to me. When you do this it will keep us from growing distant and neglecting, and it will ease any tension caused by me growing bitter over the thoughts that you don't love me because you don't kiss me five times.

Listener: You're saying that by me kissing you five times a day, you'll feel loved, accepted and secure in this relationship.

I realize that...

Speaker: I realize that you can get busy sometimes, and you tend to be focused when you're working on important projects, so kissing me might not be on your priority list on any given day.

Listener: You realize that when I don't kiss you, it's because I'm focused on important business.

What I can do is...

Speaker: What I can do is drop little hints to remind you that I look forward to and enjoy your kisses. On days when you're really pressed to get things done, I'll understand that it's not because you don't want to kiss me, it's just you don't have enough time.

Listener: You'll help me to remember by dropping hints for me to kiss you, and if work is overwhelming, you won't hold it against me if I don't kiss you five times.

I appreciate you for...

Speaker: I appreciate you for all your hard work and for how well you provide for this family. I appreciate you being a spiritual leader in this home, and I appreciate the way you serve Christ Jesus so faithfully.

Listener: You appreciate me for my work ethic, how I provide, my leadership, and my faithfulness to Christ the King.

And I look forward to...
Speaker: And I look forward to how this conversation will help us to meet needs and draw us closer together as a couple.
Listener: You're looking forward to closer relationship where I display affection that will speak love to you.

Thank you for listening.

Once the speaker has finished with the specific issue, the roles can be reversed so that the listener now becomes the speaker if they need to share anything with the spouse.

The example used as the speaker's need to address the spouse may have seemed petty and hardly anything to base discussion on, but remember that when someone shares their heart with you, even if the topic may appear trivial to you, it's a major issue in their minds. Empathy is crucial to be a healthy and mature person and for a couple to stay connected well. Empathy is the ability to share in another person's emotions, thoughts, and feelings. What's key in this important action is understanding that even though what the other person shares isn't a problem area or an issue for you, you are trying to feel what they're feeling, trying to understand what they're thinking, and experiencing the emotions they're dealing with. When you can master this technique, you can encourage, help, and communicate better than ever before.

* 12 *

RESPECT AND COMMUNICATION

Relationships aren't easy things to navigate, operate, or maintain. They take work, skill, patience, and forgiveness. In every successful relationship, there is an equation of self-sacrifice, honor, and integrity which will lead to trust and fruitfulness. The indispensible keys to a growing and maturing marriage are respect and communication. The husband and the wife need both. Because of the way God wired men, they desire respect more than communication, and that speaks love most prominently to them. Women are more social creations, and they long for communication, but they especially desire it from their husbands, and they feel loved when their husbands let them into their lives and thoughts.

Wouldn't it be nice if we could just say, "Oh, now that I know what my spouse needs I can meet it, and likewise my spouse will reciprocate by giving me what I need?"

There's only one gigantic problem with that: selfishness. Since the time of Adam and Eve's fall into sin, the human race and marriages, have experienced the detrimental effects of selfishness. People naturally want what they want, but they aren't inclined to freely give without the prospect of some kind of return. Risk and reward is being eliminated from the marriage relationship. Chivalry is on its deathbed. Self-less, sacrificial love is being replaced with "what can I get out of this relationship?"

Positive change is desperately needed in marriage. Marriage and the family are the foundational relationships for civilization. If they continue to crumble, the human race will decline. So how can change occur? It'll happen one relationship at a time. There are skills and tools to strengthen your relationship as well as habits and weapons that need disposal to prevent emotional harm. These tools when initiated and practiced properly will decrease anger escalation and invalidation where your mate's personhood or feelings are trampled. Negative interpretations will also decline where communications are skewed through wrong thinking.

In every marriage there will be conflict. It's inevitable because two different people with two different personalities, backgrounds, goals, and gifts are becoming one through holy matrimony. Different people have different ways of addressing stress, responsibility, family, and children. Who's right? Who's wrong? Who can say? Due to the differences, friction, and frustration, there is a common emotional response that will result: anger. Although anger is prevalent because of marital frustration, that emotion has been deemed as unholy. The Bible says in James 1:19, "Be angry and sin not." The Word of God doesn't forbid us from becoming angry; it's a God-given emotion. The problem results when we are angry, give in to that emotion, and start sinning. This usually happens when something happens that produces a result different from the one you desire. Anger can either flare up in spontaneous explosions, or it can be stored up and not dealt with. It's more dangerous not to deal with your anger in a healthy way; if you bottle it up it doesn't leave room for other emotions such as love and joy to be poured into your life. In a previous chapter, we considered the concept of the emotional cup. Theoretically, everyone has an emotional cup, and most always it's filled with either positive emotions or hurtful, unhealthy ones. What we allow to fill our emotional cup is what will pour out of us eventually. Forgiveness and reconciliation are factors which will clean out the unwanted emotions and give us room for the healthy, loving, and joyful emotions we long for.

In order to avoid friction in marriage, which may produce rejection or anger, each spouse has specific freedoms that are important to understand and respect. There are five freedoms by Virginia Satir, a leading family therapist and theorist, that are consistent with scripture. Every spouse has these five freedoms.

We all have the freedom to see and hear what is here, instead of what should be or will be.

When we argue, we don't deal with what is here in front of us. We are arguing about what we want, should have had, ought to have had, or the way we think things should have been. The reality is we want to talk about what is here in this present moment. What are you feeling right now rather than what you should be feeling? When you tell somebody how they should be feeling instead of realizing how they are feeling, you invalidate their emotions. In some religious settings, we almost put a sanction against our emotions.

"You are not allowed to feel that way," they say.

I ask, "Why not?"

The Lord respects how you feel. You have the right to feel the way you want to feel. He may not agree with what you do with those feelings, but He always respects your feelings. We should give the same grace to our fellow man or woman.

We all have the freedom to say what we feel and think instead of how others think you should feel or think.

I don't have the right to tell my wife, "I don't care how you think about a certain issue. You should be thinking this way." I'm not considering her feelings. What I'd be doing is pushing my agenda. My wife has the right to think what she thinks. Even if she's wrong, she still has the right to think that way; however, I don't have to agree with her.

There are times it can be tough and there are times it can be easy, but it's possible to make other people think what you think. We can actually convert them over to doing and thinking things our way. They may cave into the pressure, capitulate, and do things your way, but in the long term, they're going to go back to their way of thinking. Forcing someone to agree to think a certain way takes away their freedom to choose. But when you show them the truth about your way of thinking, or help them to understand the truth in such a way they can internalize it, they make the ultimate decision to remain the way they are or choose a better path. They have that freedom.

We have the freedom to feel the way we feel instead of the how we ought to.

This is self-explanatory. You have the right to feel what you feel. For example, if you are angry about something, and I think it's stupid for you to be angry about it, it's irrelevant what I think. The way you feel is angry, and I'll have to respect that fact. If you feel rejected because of something I did, even though I didn't mean to make you feel that way, I'm going to respect your feelings. I'll be sad when you feel rejected because I love you and don't want you to feel that way. Proactively, I'll minister to that hurt, and confess that I didn't communicate something correctly. If I were to say you shouldn't be feeling that way, it wouldn't change or improve anything. The reality is that you do feel that way.

We have the freedom to ask for what we want instead of waiting for permission.

Now this gets to the core of a personality trait called assertiveness. We all have the right to be assertive. Assertiveness is healthy. Research shows the more assertive a person is the more self-confidence they have in a relationship. The less assertive you become, the more you avoid decisions and conflicts, and the more likely your partner will try to control you or dominate you.

What is assertiveness? It is defined as the ability to ask for what I want and to share my thoughts and feelings. It's all right for me to say, "I disagree with what you're saying," or "I need a hug."

Being assertive is good, but over time, people stop communicating assertively and instead start thinking assertively. We assume people should know what we want. Don't assume. Ask for what you want. The Bible says, "You have not because you don't ask" (James 4:2).

Let me caution you. If you want something, don't demand it. There's a big difference between asking and demanding.

"Can I get a hug," I can ask. "I'm really feeling dejected right now, and a hug would cheer me up."

But if I sense you're choosing not to listen, I can demand a hug, but I'm no longer being assertive. I'm being aggressive. You don't want that. Everybody's got the right to ask for what they want without waiting for permission, but remember that the other party has the right not to grant your request. The key word here is respect. We need to respect others' requests, but we should also respect others' responses.

We have the freedom to take risk

Life is full of risks and rewards. Many never get to the reward because they fear what the risk will cost. This is a relationship freedom we all have, but one many choose not to employ. We have the freedom to take risks on our own behalf instead of choosing only the secure and not rocking the boat. In pre-marital and marriage relationships, this reluctance is prevalent. One person doesn't want to "rock the boat," so they don't talk about a troublesome issue. In order to keep the peace now, they won't talk about the problem, but sweep it under the rug, and hope it'll go away. It won't go away, and the temporary calm you settle for now, will build up to big conflict later. You want the relationship to feel good and you desire a level of confidence, so you won't deal with anything, but the issue you ignore now won't be tolerated four or five years into the marriage. You have the freedom to take risks because sometimes healthy conflict will make sure your relationship is intimate, thriving, growing, and strong.

The key to it all

The door to a vibrant relationship is opened by a single key. That key is a powerful word we hear a lot but have little idea of what it means. Respect. What is respect? Its simplest and most profound definition is being thoughtful of another's feelings. Hearing that definition may bring back painful memories of what others had done to you or how you've responded to others. That's all right because regret is natural. The great thing about each day is that it's a fresh slate, and we don't have to wallow in our past failures or disappointments.

You can tell people are respectful by their behavior. Respect is always indicated by what you do and how you treat other people. If I treat my wife in such a way that it invalidates her or hurts her feelings, I am being disrespectful. Whether I like what you say or do, if I respond in a way that's not thoughtful of your feelings, I'm being disrespectful. Just because I disagree with you—or even if I don't like you—it doesn't mean I can't be respectful to you. People are varied, and there may be personality differences, but whenever I'm in their presence, I can always choose to treat them with respect. You may never see me eating lunch with certain folks, and you may never see me over at their house, but I will always treat them with respect because that's my obligation before the Lord. There are some people who are very dysfunctional and disrespectful people, and they will treat you with disrespect. But is that the reputation you want to have? When you deal with a disrespectful person, do you want to respond to them likewise? Of course not. The Lord Jesus himself said, "Do for others what you would like them to do for you" (Matthew 7:12).

We can choose to be either respectful or disrespectful in a heated battle. If you give in to that anger, you'll start making excuses for your own behavior saying, "I'm being disrespectful because you're being disrespectful to me." One of the core needs of our hearts is respect. When you treat someone disrespectfully, you aren't ministering to a core need, and everyone wants to be treated respectfully.

Here's something dangerous to watch out for in your marriage: if you don't treat your mate respectfully, in the long run, someone else will. When respect is coming from somebody else, when it should be coming from you, their two hearts are going to join. After all, why would I give my heart to you, love you, and make myself vulnerable to you when you treat me in a disrespectful way?

Pay attention! In communication, respect is not about agreeing. A hallmark of healthy relationships is that there's mutual respect even in the midst of relational storms. Now if respect is shown by your behavior, your mouth is the megaphone that broadcasts the intent of your behavior. Your words verbalize the feelings of your heart. Communication is key for the survival of any relationship, and it is absolutely vital in conflict resolution.

When differences arise in relationships, how we solve them? I will go into depth about that in the following chapter.

YOUR EMOTIONAL TRASHCAN

All of us have the capacity in our very core to love since we are made in the image of God. But in relationships, there can be unwanted blows that can cause pain, hurt, anger, and disappointment. These arouse fear that will increase inside of you. The feelings of love, pleasure, and tenderness begin to get suppressed and are covered over by feelings such as disappointment, rejection, helplessness, hopelessness, despair, as well as feeling unloved, unappreciated, and unimportant. Nobody wants to feel like that, so the blanket feeling of pain overshadows all those emotions, and it's expressed through anger.

Anger is what is called a secondary emotion. How many people like to feel rejected? How about helpless, hopeless, or abandoned? We don't want to experience these emotions and want to dispose of them, and anger is our emotional trashcan.

What do you do with a trashcan at home? Typically, you put trash in your trashcan. Sounds simple enough. So what's the basic purpose of your trashcan? It's a place where you dispose of the things you don't want to see, smell, or experience. You put a lid on it, and place it out of sight. As long as you have the lid on, you don't have to experience the trash. God actually wired us the same way. It's possible to take painful emotions and lock them away. You can actually put them in what I call your emotional trashcan. Each of us has one. So if I feel rejected or abandoned, I can lock that feeling away by throwing it away, but I have to cap this lid because as long as I don't have a lid on it, I can see, smell, or experience it. This is called "stuffing down your feelings."

You've got to uncap this emotional trashcan. There's only one emotion strong enough to lock away those feelings and it's called anger. Anger is always fueled by something or somebody else, not your stuffed emotions.

The Bible says we can be angry, but it warns us not to sin because of that anger. Be careful. Don't do something negative or sinful with the anger. The Lord knows the reality of your anger is that you're restraining pain underneath it. But if you get into a sinful behavior pattern, you're taking your anger and acting it out, which causes more pain for you and your relationships. When your anger becomes sinful, you aren't able to step back and examine the emotions causing it. "What is this anger really about?" "What is it that I'm really feeling underneath this anger?"

Anger is the safer emotion to express. I'd rather feel angry than abandoned or rejected. You and I were socialized from the day we were born by society and our parents to go right to the emotion of anger. When you felt hurt or disappointed, you're asked, "What are you feeling that way for? Are you a weakling?" So what other response do we have than to turn to anger right away? In today's culture, we are told not to get angry. So you don't want to experience the pain, but you aren't supposed to have an outlet through healthy anger. You are being taught to further repress your anger, to not experience it. Can anyone be so in control of all their emotions that they don't feel them? I remind you that Jesus Christ, when you look in the scriptures, never repressed or pushed away His emotions. He always experienced His emotions as He felt them in that moment whether it was sorrow, joy, grief, or dread; however, He did it without sinning. In the garden of Gethsemane, Jesus Christ experienced fear when He knew He was about to suffer the full wrath of God for the sins of mankind and the complete abandonment of His Father on the cross. He requested, "Father, let this cup pass from me." He experienced the fear, but He didn't give in to it. He went on to say, "nevertheless, not my will but Thine be done."

When Christ was angry about something, He did not sin. Anger in itself is not a sin, but when we get angry, we give into it and produce sin. So understand that anger is nothing more than a cover for fear and pain—physical, psychological, or emotional.

Why do you think fear is a core human emotion? After all, we all experience it, some in various ways, and others in many ways. This issue goes all the way back to the Garden of Eden. The first two new human experiences at the fall of mankind were shame and fear.

Shame says, "There's something wrong with me. You wouldn't like me if you know me."

Fear pushes us away from a relationship. Fear proclaims, "You might have rejected me or discovered a shameful aspect of my past, and because of that I can't let you close to me again because if I let you into me you might hurt me again."

"You might reject me," you say, "And I'm not willing to let you hurt me anymore." Do you hear the fear in that statement?

What happens in relationships over time is fear, pain, and anger begin to build, and the person is living with this accumulation of hurt in their hearts. Want to know why they can't get back to the feelings of love, trust, and romance? They can't feel those emotions because of the overwhelming crowding of fear, pain, and anger.

One of the mistakes I made for many years as a therapist was trying to get people to regain their original pleasant feelings for each other without dealing with the pain and heartache that drove those feelings into hiding. The stench won't go away until you take out the trash.

There was a couple in our church that had been married for 20 years. The wife held a lot of anger. Her husband was insensitive and uncaring toward her. When they would argue, he would push her and call her many deriding names.

Of course, they didn't start their marriage this way. They started out in love, having dreams of living happily ever after. But like many marriages, the mirage shatters and reality sets in. What reality is that? The reality is that a couple consists of two different people with two different histories, personalities, and hang-ups. Maintaining the feelings of love involves hard work. Frustration occurs when that dream isn't occurring like we'd envisioned, and unfortunately, this turns mates against each other. The differences and unique qualities enjoyed during courting or dating now become points of contention, and attitudes, actions, and words turn sour.

When I was counseling this couple, the hurt seemed so deep for the wife that there seemed no way to reconcile their differences. It was a tough frustrating case for me, because I knew if I could just get their "Us-ness" back, that they could handle the minor issues with communication and forgiveness. But she simply wouldn't respond.

A friend and fellow counselor understood my quandary and told me, "She's not going to get to a point where she opens back up to her husband and restore that marriage."

"Why not?" I asked.

"She's got too much hurt and pain in her to experience any other emotions."

I knew what the problem was, and I felt like I knew the solution. There are two things that create intimacy in a relationship: Physical closeness and emotional openness.

In the next counseling session, I had the husband come up close to his wife and hold her—the physical closeness. Then I told the wife, "Open up emotionally to your husband. Tell him everything in your heart. Share your true feelings and don't hold back. He needs to hear it, and you need to release it.

"Husband, all you are allowed to do is hold her and listen to her pain and care."

I knew she couldn't get back to her feelings of love and openness toward her man until she dealt with all the painful emotions filling up her emotional jug. So while he held her in that intimate position she yelled at him, pouring out a stream of anger and fear, and calling him a few choice words. All he was doing was saying you're right and I'm wrong, and I am so sorry over and over again. After an hour and fifteen minute barrage, she finally became quiet, looking exhausted, and then said, "But I still love you."

Now they could begin rebuilding, but not until then. But isn't it a shame that they had to go through almost twenty years of marriage or distance and stuffing emotions when if they had practiced physical closeness and emotional openness they would never have had their emotional jugs filling up with destructive and poisoning emotions.

Beware the pitfalls

How is it that two people can fall in love, get married, and then have their whole relationship begin to crumble over time? Where is the starting point where we actually start hurting each other?

Before we get to the hurtful communication styles, let me summarize the typical stages that a relationship goes through.

The first stage is the "**illusion stage.**" No, we're not talking about magic tricks or disappearing acts. What this stage involves is the "fairy tale" or fantasy image of your mind concerning your partner. In this stage, each partner is perfect and loveable. There's never going to be any problems. Everything's going to be wonderful. You may be thinking, *"Everybody else may have an illusion problem in their relationship, but this definitely can't apply to us."* You're in an illusion, and we've all done it at one point or another. There's something loveable about your partner, but there's some bad about them too. There's good and bad about all of us.

The "illusion stage" is followed by the "**disappointment stage.**" This is when you realize your mate isn't perfect, and you become disillusioned. You may think things like, *"I just never thought she'd act that way." "Why is* *he acting that way, he never did while we were engaged?" "You never showed me this or told me this when we were dating."*

Reality starts to set in and your illusion is shattered.

From here you move to the "**confusion stage**." When the illusion dissipates and reality sets in, your dream and vision for the relationship seems to crumble, and doubts permeate your thinking and attitudes. *"Do I really love her?" "Will this guy meet my needs? Does he even have a desire to know how I feel?"* Thoughts turn inward and hopelessness bears down on you. You begin to think that there is peace outside of this relationship, and you may even see someone other than your spouse as the hope to having your needs met.

Marriage is tough. A successful one takes hard work. It may not seem encouraging to hear the negative things that happen among couples, but it's what happens frequently. If I'm going to give you a route to drive up a mountain, I'm going to warn you about the dangers along the way. I hope you enjoy the ride through the mountains, but "be careful around this curve," "watch out for the big trucks in the other lane," and "slow down around these slippery areas." In marriage you should have a nice trip, but be cautious and careful concerning the dangers.

Finishing up the stages, if we're not careful we end up at the "**power-struggle stage**." The relationship begins taking on aspects of dirty fighting and selfish behaviors because of poor communication. At this point, one or both spouses look to get their own needs met. They remain in their house, but live as roommates. They sleep in the same bed, but there is no connection, no intimacy, and no bonding.

But when you dare to have dialogue, when you challenge yourselves to face the issues and even get into conflict about differing views and opinions, the disconnect can't last long. Conflict occurs when a relationship is threatened. Conflict is always meant to draw us together. When you war through issues that divide, you'll go to bed with a deep sense of intimacy and connectedness, and you'll think, *"I didn't mind that conflict because of what it did to draw us closer together."* But let me remember you: conflict is meant to defeat whatever enemy is afflicting your relationship; it's not to tear down each other.

Warning! Here are hurtful things to avoid when in conflict:

Dirty fighting techniques

This is when you bring up more than one issue at a time. You tell your spouse you need to talk about a certain issue or problem, but as the conversation progresses, you are no longer addressing the original issue. The talk about one problem was used as a springboard into other complaints or dislikes.

Bullying

You do this by screaming, exploding, and intimidating your spouse.

Contempt

This is where you turn vitriol toward your mate, saying things like "You just think you're so smart, don't you?" "I'm so disgusted with you sometimes."

Criticism

This is simply where you start tearing down the other person. "Things would have worked if you had done it this way instead." "Well, you're not perfect. You just think you are." Sometimes the criticism can lead from tearing down to lying. You'll also humiliate by labeling, saying, "you're just like your mother." "You're a moron." "I can't believe I married a clown." Mocking could also be involved, mimicking your mate in such a way as to make them look like a caricature of their real selves.

Mind reading

"I know what you're going to say." "You think I'm the worst person in the world." This also leads into psychoanalyzing. "The reason you're doing this is because you're just like your father. In many ways you are your father."

Of course there are the other "power-struggle games" designed to get one up on the other, such as name calling or barking orders. One can play dumb, saying "I don't get what you're saying." Another can be utterly demanding, "I'm the one in charge here. I'm the head of this home." Sarcasm and blaming are other notorious tools used in dirty fighting.

Conflict naturally produces stress. To understand how to analyze the actions caused by stress, remember the brain does one of three things when it feels stress: it goes to a **fight** mode, a **flight** mode, or a **freeze** mode.

If you give into the **fight mode** you automatically move toward blaming. In this mode not only does your voice rise but your body gets active also. You may approach and begin gesturing with your hands, or start pointing. "This isn't about what I do. This is about you. You know you're the one in the wrong!" Your brain is producing this energy because you feel stress in your relationship. In the fight mode, your objective becomes to attack. There is a difference between disagreeing and fighting. Disagreeing is when your points of view don't seem to match up, causing friction. Fighting happens when stress enters your relationship, and you become bent on hurting the other person physically or verbally.

Some don't go into fight mode; they don't like that kind of heated conflict. Instead they slip into the **flight mode**; they'd rather run away from the friction. These people are called placaters. Since placaters don't want to deal with the conflict, they'll do anything to appease the situation. Typically, you'll see them sit down and say, "You're right. You're exactly right. I am an imbecile. You know you're always right, honey. What can I do to fix the problem?" What you're communicating to yourself and your spouse is what you say and what you feel in this relationship isn't important. This isn't healthy, and long term, it can be destructive.

Another way the flight mode displays itself is when a person takes on the role of a distracter. When acting out this scenario, the distracter still wants to avoid the conflict, but they do it in a less self-demeaning way.

Let's say I want to talk to about something that happened in the house. "Honey, can we talk?"

Instantly, the spouse's fight mode fires up, and she starts blaming me for things that may have happened weeks before and had nothing to do with what happened today. Maybe she's attacking in self-defense, maybe anger, but I back off.

"It's not that important anyway," I say, then extend the distraction. "Hey, how about we go out to dinner?"

You don't deal with the issue, you simply move away from it.

Lastly, we have the **freeze mode**. I also call it the computer mode. In the computer mode you shut down emotionally; what you think or say isn't important, and what I think and say isn't important. What's important is the information.

Let's say my wife and I get into an argument. Instead of going into fight or flight mode, I shut off my emotions and mechanically speak only the facts.

"Well, no honey, you see, if you'd be the wife you're supposed to be according to Ephesians 5:23-24, you'd be submissive to me, but since you're not submissive to me, there's nothing we can do here. I'm trying to be the husband you want me to be, but I can't be the husband I'm supposed to be because you're not being the submissive wife you're supposed to be."

Do you sense the detachment? You shut down emotionally, you leave the relationship emotionally, and you're sticking to the facts.

If you get into an attack (fight) mode, a placating (flight) mode, or a computer (freeze) mode, you'll never solve problems. What we want to do is sit face-to-face, knee-to-knee, physically close and emotionally open, and that's why we practice the dialogue guide. You train your brain so you control it even in times when you feel like running, fighting, or going unresponsive. If you stick to your dialogue skills you will actually control what your brain's doing neuro-chemically, you won't give into stress responses, and you'll actually communicate well. This cannot be overemphasized: Communication is the key to successful relationships.

The behind-the-scenes reasons

Threatening and using cold logic is the whole idea of hiding from our emotions. We've talked about the pitfalls to communication, and the ways different people respond to the stress that occurs in conflict. Now I'm going to draw a picture in your mind so you can see how this works and how people think when they react in any given mode.

Imagine a circle. I'm going to divide it into three separate and equal wedge-shaped parts. Can you visualize that? One section represents me, my thoughts, and my feelings. The second part is my spouse, her thoughts, and her feelings. The third part stands for the content—the issues we're fighting about.

Now taking the image, let me show you how each mode executes the individual's way of thinking and coping with the stress of conflict. If you are placating—the run away mode—what I'm saying is "what I think and feel in the relationship doesn't matter." So they cross themselves off—their wedge of the equation—and decide their thoughts and feelings are worthless. That way of thinking is flawed, but that's their stress response.

If I'm in the blaming mode, the other person is getting the "X." You are saying, "I will cross you out, and I will do whatever it takes to get what I want."

Responding to stress by going into the computer mode, leads to a person's body actually stiffens up. They go rigid, shut down emotionally, and spout information, facts, and data. What they are saying is, "Neither you nor I are important. All that matters are the facts."

The distracter's view of things is the worst. The distracter says, "What I think and feel isn't important. What you think and feel isn't important. The issue isn't important. Let's just not deal with it."

All these are destructive ways to handle conflict stress.

Beware of the more subtle and passive ways as well. You can complain. You can disqualify your actions by saying things like, "I didn't mean to do that." That's just another way of dirty fighting. So are statements like, "I can never remember what you asked for."

When you "drag your feet" about something important, it's a passive sign of a power struggle. "I couldn't help being late."

Keeping score also is treacherous. "If I remember right, I think I've done more for you in these first two years of marriage than you've done for me."

Making excuses casts blame on others, and deflects responsibility from you. "I started calling you names because you made me so mad." Just because you get mad doesn't mean you have the right to put anybody down. What you do is not somebody else's fault. No one has the power to make you do anything. You choose to do it. That's the bottom line.

Playing martyr is another form of dirty fighting. "Look how hard I work. Look at all I do for you. I sacrifice so much, I go to work all the day and what do you do? You don't do anything, and I can't even get a simple thank you."

Playing the "poor me" game is a form of manipulation. "...You know, I guess I'm just a terrible wife." This line leads the couple away from the real subject into making the other spouse think they must rescue you.

"Oh no, you're a good wife."

"No, I'm not. If I was this wouldn't be an issue, and you'd be happier with me. But sometimes I think I'm not good enough for you."

"Oh honey, you are good enough for me."

Do you see how the pressure has been displaced from the issue to the spouse? You're weighing down your spouse with all the stuff they were confronting you about. So instead of talking about the issue and bringing healing to the relationship, they're talking about their spouse's problem and feeling they must come to the rescue. It's a subtle power tactic to shift the issue away.

Pretending your partner is always being unreasonable is called stone walling. The silent treatment is part of this—not talking to your mate and withholding conversation, love, or affection.

These are all the things to watch out for in communicating to each other. The dirty fighting and power struggles are never conducive for a happy, successful relationship. It's one thing to know that these things can happen in a relationship; it's another thing to do some introspection and to be willing to purposefully mature by changing the things you're doing wrong. Nobody's perfect, and no one person causes all the problems in the relationship. For the next five minutes, I want you to write down at least three things that you see yourself doing to your mate when you're in conflict. I also want you to write down three things your mate does. Take your lists and share them with each other, and if you don't understand what they mean by that, use your dialogue if you need to. This is about growing in insight.

Aristotle said this, "Anyone can be angry. That is easy. But to be angry with the right person, to the right degree, at the right time, for the right purpose and in the right way, that is not easy."

I may be angry with my wife and take it out on the kids. Something at work could make me angry and I'll come home and yell my wife, and my anger could come out disproportionate to the issue.

Ephesians 4:31-32 says this, "And grieve not the Holy Spirit of God whereby you are sealed unto the day of salvation. Get rid of all bitterness, rage, anger, harsh words, and slander, as well as all types of malicious behavior. Instead, be kind to each other, tenderhearted, forgiving one another, just as God through Christ forgave you."

* 13 *

WHO'S MOST IMPORTANT?

What can be the most frustrating, confusing, aggravating relationship in the human experience? What can be the most intriguing, pleasant, satisfying human relationship you can be blessed with? It's not surprising that there's one answer to both these questions: the adventure called marriage. Of all the other relationships in life, marriage demands the most, rewards the most, and can hurt the most.

How can marriage be the biggest blessing for some and become the worst curse for others? What enables some marriages to thrive while others quickly unravel? There is a fantastic key that is essential to marriage. Without it they stagnate and die. With it, they grow, mature, and flourish. What's that key? Figure out who is the most important person in the marriage and do what pleases them. Now that I've got your attention, you may be wondering, "Who in this marriage is the most important?"

Most husbands might be thinking, "I'm the most important one. I'm the breadwinner who pays the mortgage and the bills. I make sure my family has a roof over their head, food on the table, and clothes on their back."

Most wives might be thinking, "I'm the most important one. I am the organizer, the cook, and the one who takes care of the kids. I do all the small errands that make this household run smoothly. If I didn't do all I do our lives would be chaotic."

May I say that neither the husband nor the wife is the most important person in the marriage?

If you're thinking spiritually, you're thinking, "God is the glue that holds the marriage together. It's His precepts and His blessings that hold our relationship together." Without the Lord, marriage would be hollow and lack the fulfilling purpose God designed it for. But for our illustration, we are going to let the Lord step aside so I can show you who really is the most important person in the marriage.

You might be thinking, "If we're not talking about God, the husband, or the wife, who could be the most important person in the marriage?"

Before I answer that question, let me ask you a few more. In an earlier chapter we touched on this, but I want to expand on a particular thought. Written in Genesis 2:24 the Bible says, Therefore shall a man leave his father and mother, and shall cleave unto his wife: and they shall be one flesh.

What does the Bible mean when it says "one flesh?"

"Could it mean both of you are in agreement?"

Not necessarily. You could be in agreement with somebody and not be one flesh.

"Could it mean you are always in close proximity?"

Not at all. You can be physically and emotionally close to many people, but you wouldn't consider that being one flesh with them.

"Could it mean you are going to be of one mind?"

The answer is no. In a one-flesh relationship, you don't lose your identity or your individuality.

Stick with me; this is going somewhere good.

Let me ask you this question in a different manner. If you know what "becoming one flesh" means, do you experience it just because you know what it is? The answer, of course, is no. Just because I can define it for you doesn't mean I actually have it.

If you had a one-flesh relationship, how would you know you had it?

Does it mean you won't have conflict? No. You can have one-fleshness and still have a degree of conflict.

The only way you can know if you have a one-flesh relationship is if you

feel it. Now some of you might be thinking, "That sounds a bit superficial and shallow." But think about it. If you've got anger, how do you know you have anger? You feel it. If you've got bitterness in your heart, how do you know you've got it? You feel it. If you're happy or excited, how do you know? You feel it.

When a husband and wife become one flesh, both of you are bringing your strengths. Some people may think, *Well, I don't have any strengths.* Yes, you do. You may not realize it yet, but we all have several. We have parts that are good, we have specific skills, gifts, and abilities which God gave to you.

You also bring weaknesses and limitations into the relationship. In a one-flesh relationship, one's strengths can compensate for another's weaknesses.

Into the relationship, you are also bringing your hopes, your dreams, your desires, and expectations of the future. You may be hoping that he is this type of husband. You may be dreaming of her being this type of wife. You are bringing with you your expectations of what marriage is supposed to be, what sex is going to be like, and how you're going to parent your children.

What makes us one flesh?

It's not when we agree to do life together, walk down an aisle, and stand in front of a preacher who does the ceremony and pronounces, "Man and wife, you can kiss."

It doesn't happen when we finally have sex.

Having a one-flesh relationship is when the most important person in that marriage is introduced.

So who is the most important person in a marriage?

The best and most contemporary way of describing a one-flesh relationship is the word "Us-ness." The thing about us-ness is that it's more important than the husband or the wife. The husband is different from the wife. The wife is different from the husband. The most important person in the marriage relationship is not him or her; it's **Us**.

In the sense of Us-ness, there is a spiritual aspect, a relational emotional component that is linked with God's principles. If we lived the principles the Lord created to make our marriage enjoyable, if we lived out what the Word of God directs, our brains will begin to function in a way that'll allow us to feel the results. If I'm thinking love and forgiveness (which are key for a lasting marriage), then my brain will produce the actions that go with that thought pattern.

Contrariwise, if I have anger, bitterness, and resentment in my thought life, my brain is going to produce that in my actions. But if I practice Biblical principles like resolution, and let go of bitterness and resentment, my brain produces positive feelings like joy and peace. If I do what the Lord says through His Word, my brain produces something better for me. By the way, these precepts work for unredeemed people also. Unredeemed people can forgive others and let go of bitterness and resentment too. The difference between them and those who are saved is that they will suffer a Christ-less eternity if they don't repent. But in terms of a somewhat relational health, they will have success if they practice biblical principles. Biblical principles will work for anybody who uses them.

I'm going to argue that the most important person in your marriage is this person called Us. It's not me who's most important. It's not my wife. The most important part is this thing called Us-ness. I make all my decisions based on what is not best for me or what's best for my wife; I make all my decisions according to what's best for Us. When Us is most important, I start doing strange things like dying to my selfishness. For me? No. For my wife? No. For whom? Us.

I begin living the biblical principle of esteeming others more highly than myself, and I wouldn't esteem my wife higher than myself of her sake; I do it for Us.

You may be thinking, "This still needs a little more explaining."

Here's why nurturing Us is so important. If I compromise on something in marriage and say, "Okay, I'll give in, and you can have it your way," what happens? You feel like you lost and your spouse won. Pay close attention to this next statement. A healthy marriage doesn't work that way. Whenever one person wins, and the other loses, you both lose because you sacrifice your Us-ness. You sacrifice this thing called one-fleshness. How many people does it take to make Us? Two. So what happens if all my decisions are based on what's best for us, and I esteem my spouse more highly than myself, not for her sake but the sake of Us? With me being part of this equation, if I deny self for the sake of Us, I also give to me.

Some guy might be thinking, "Well, what if I'm doing this stuff, and one day I come home frisky and ask, 'How bout tonight?' She turns and says, 'No. I've got a headache. It's been a rotten day at work.' Is Us supposed to be me doing all the giving with her doing all the taking, with her selectively deciding when to give back?"

Of course that answer is no, but in this instance you are presented with a choice.

If you say, "I'm sick and tired of you being tired all the time. You never want to have sex." At that point you are making a choice for you.

But what does it sound like if you're making a choice for Us?

"Sounds like you've had a rough day. I just want you to know I love you. What can I do to help?"

You might be thinking to yourself now, *I've made a decision for Us, but my needs aren't being met.* That's the selfish thought pattern that always proves so destructive in the marriage relationship. The reason why needs aren't met between spouses is because one is thinking, *I'm not going to meet their needs, because they're not meeting mine.* Do you think the other spouse is thinking the same thing? Because of that selfish mindset, neither do anything for the other, and both live in misery and contempt.

But men when you take the initiative to meet her needs for the sake of Us, she, too, will be moved to make a decision which will benefit Us.

After ministering comfort and concern to her, her response might be similar to this: "Listen, I know it's rough for you right now, and I know you want to be close to me, and I want to be close to you too, but it's not a good night. When you come home from work tomorrow, big boy, we'll make something happen."

When you give to Us, you win, even if you deny self. When you choose to esteem your mate higher than yourself for the sake of Us, you're still giving to you. The reason why is because the Us-ness stays around. You may not get your needs met every time you have them, but you will have them met when there's Us-ness because the two of you are striving to keep the relationship nurtured and vibrant. If you shatter the Us-ness, the reality is your needs won't be met. It'll be each person striving for their own selfish agendas instead of for the benefit of the Us-ness relationship. You always know when you've got it because you can feel the harmony, the peace, the desire to bless the other person, not because you feel you have to, but because you want to. You can also feel when you don't have it. You can feel the tension, the distance, and the disconnectedness. If everything you do is based on what's best for us, you are going to win.

My wife and I got into a fight once. She gave her point. I gave mine. She reiterated hers, and I did the same. You could feel the tension, and, at that point, the Us-ness wasn't there anymore. I was going to win this fight because I knew I was right. The problem was she, too, knew she was right. So I did the typical male thing by walking away and withdrawing. Since I was frustrated about the whole thing I went downstairs to play computer games—this is my form of escape—but I could still feel the tension in our relationship. I could feel it in the room and the entire house.

After about 30 minutes of being locked away, a thought comes to mind, *Don't I teach this stuff? Of course, I do. I need to get back upstairs and get our Us-ness back because I hate the tension.* So I went back upstairs and found her, but this time my goal wasn't to be right, it was to rejuvenate the one-flesh relationship. I hate the loss of the Us-ness.

"You can feel the tension, can't you?" I asked.

"I can."

"You know why it's here?"

"Because you think you're right." She said.

"The problem is I know I'm right, and you know you're right. How about we agree to disagree instead of being disconnected?"

"Okay," she answered. "Let's do that."

Within three minutes, guess what showed back up. Us. We could feel the connectedness again. It wasn't important enough for me to be right for the sake of killing off our Us-ness.

Everything you do must be based on what is best for the Us-ness in the marriage. Us is not me and it's not her. I'll give you an example. I don't like the mall. My wife, on the other hand, loves to go to the mall to shop or for no other reason than to look around. If you see me at the mall, believe this—It's not me who's there, it's Us. There's something about walking hand-in-hand that makes it all worth it. I'm not there for the mall. I'm there for her. She loves the mall, but she also loves the fact that I'm there by her side. Even if I don't prefer something, Us does because it nurtures the love and connectedness of the relationship. So it's not about me, and it's not about her. It's about creating and fostering a one-flesh connection.

The Ultimate Third Person

Now I've got to invite the Lord back into this equation because it's important that you understand that there are going to be times when you don't feel the Us-ness. Circumstances, miscommunication, or a shattering of trust can rip the Us-ness apart at the seams, and it's only the Lord and his Word that can bring healthy reconciliation and healing back to that relationship.

I see a sad trend among Christians after doing nearly three decades of counseling with Christians. Christians have caught up to and just about passed the unredeemed, non-Christian couples in dissolution of relationships and in divorce. Lost (non-Christian) people seem to be a lot more accepting than Christians, and much less judgmental.

As I've counseled Christians for more than a decade, I hear increasingly more tell me, "My 'saved' friends judge and criticize me more than my 'lost' friends."

"That's because they're being self-righteous and pious like the Pharisees were," I'd say.

Because of that trend, the church in the United States is losing its impact in reaching unbelievers with the Good News of Jesus Christ. Self-righteous swagger added to worldly living produces no desire for people to want to trust the same God you say you follow.

The unredeemed look at some Christians and say, "You've got the same divorce rates we've got. You've got the same amount of domestic violence we've got. You've got the same amount of alcoholism and pornography we've got. You're no different than us, so why should I listen to you? And if you live just as badly as I do, what right do you have to tell me how to behave?"

I'm thankful for churches that are trying to set a standard and say, "Christians should live up to that standard."

But let's bring this closer to home, literally. The church is only as strong as the families that are part of it. Of course, the church is a hospital for the downhearted and soul sick, but those who love the Lord and serve

Him should be the example and the light. Our Lord Jesus Christ saved us from the wrath of God, the bondage of Satan, and the influence of sin. We Christians who live by the power of the Holy Spirit have the privilege and the responsibility to help a hurting world. But the foundation of a strong church begins with strong relationships: first with our Lord and Savior Jesus Christ, then with our spouse. The biblical mandate for both husband and wife is in Ephesians 5:21-25: "You will submit to one another out of reverence for Christ. You wives will submit to your husbands as you do to the Lord. For a husband is the head of the wife as Christ is the head of his body, the church: he gave his life to be her Savior. As the church submits to Christ, so you wives must submit to your husband in everything.

And you husbands must love your wives with the same love Christ showed the church. He gave his life for her to make her holy and clean, washed in baptism and God's Word."

The key to this passage is in verse 21. The Bible tells each spouse to submit to one another, then it goes on to explain how. To submit means that each spouse will yield their power over to the other. That means you make a conscious choice to die to yourself for the sake of the other person's best. Wives are exhorted to encourage their men to lead, while men are encouraged to love and sacrifice for their wives.

Because of some circumstances in certain relationships, or even because you might have a rebellious heart, you may say, "Well, I don't feel like doing what the Bible says. I don't feel like my spouse deserves that kind of treatment. Since they mess up all the time, neglect what's important, or don't act the way I want them to, I just don't have those feelings of love."

What I'm about to say will most likely make or break the relationship which the two of you found so important at one time that you decided to be together 'until death do you part.' You know when you have a one-flesh relationship—the Us-ness—because you feel it. But in order to attain and to maintain the Us-ness in your marriage, you don't live by your feelings; you live by convictions and commitment. There will be many times you don't feel the Us-ness in your marriage. That's when I make the choice that I'm going to love, respect, and honor my spouse. When you commit yourself to the love relationship, you rebuild the bridge to Us-ness again and the feelings of love. You know it's real love when you invest in your relationship even when you don't feel like it.

When we live by our feelings we live according to our basest human nature. The greatest human expression is love, but remember love is not a feeling, although you can feel it. Love is an action word. The reason many marriages are dissolving is because they're relying on a feeling instead of a sturdy decision to love your spouse as Christ loved you. Choosing to love in difficult situations is impossible. That's where the Lord comes into the picture. We have all the wisdom, spiritual riches, and tools we need to excel in our marriage relationship if we trust Christ and His Word. We have the Holy Spirit of God living in us as Christians, and if God has never lost a battle and never given up, He definitely wouldn't want us to give up on our marriage. He gives us wisdom if we listen. He teaches us to forgive since He's forgiven and suffered so much for each of us. He shows us success, because He defeated death, Hell, and the grave to gain a relationship with us. He showed us love through selflessness when He experienced shame, pain, and torment alone so that we wouldn't have to.

Christ had the choice whether or not to suffer eternal Hell when He did nothing wrong so that we humans with rebellious, sinful hearts could be cleansed and forgiven so we wouldn't have to perish forever. Because He loved us so much, He chose the bitter consequences of suffering for us so that we could enjoy a relationship with Him forever.

Remember how it felt to be in love? Remember the expectation of the wedding day? You didn't marry each other with the hopes of being bitter and disconnected. You chose to love each other, trust God, and do the hard work of putting aside any selfish agendas to reach the joy of the Us-ness relationship. Never give up. It'll be worth all the trials when you get there. You will be glad you did.

* 14 *

INGREDIENTS FOR INTIMACY

Relationships are complex and confusing. Often times we overcomplicate them. So before we get into the ingredients for intimacy, let's get a laugh from the straightforward responses of children questioned on relationships.

What is the proper age to marry?

Judy, age 8, said, "Eighty-four, because at that age you don't have to work and you can spend all your time loving each other."

Tommy, age 5, said, "Once I'm done with kindergarten I'm going to find me a wife, but not before."

When is it appropriate to kiss someone?

Jim, age 10, said, "You should never kiss a girl unless you have enough bucks to buy her a big ring and a DVD player because she'll want to watch movies of the wedding."

Kelly, age 9, said, "Never kiss in front of other people. It's embarrassing if anyone sees you, but if nobody's looking, I might try with a handsome boy, but just for a few hours."

Is it better to be single or married?

Lynette, age 9, said, "It's better for girls to be single, but not boys. Boys need someone to clean up after them."

Kenny, age 7, said, "It gives me a headache just thinking about it. I'm just a kid. I don't need that kind of trouble."

What is it like to fall in love?

Jean, age 9, responded, "It's like an avalanche where you have to run for your life!"

Leo, age 7, said, "If falling in love is anything like learning to spell, I don't want to do it. It takes too long to learn, and I don't have much time."

Do you have any opinions on being in love?

Anita, age 8, said, "I'm in favor of love as long as it doesn't happen while the cartoons are on TV."

Regina, age 10, said, "I'm not rushing into being in love. I'm finding 4th grade hard enough."

How do you make love last?

Roger, age 8, said, "Don't forget your wife's name. She hates that."

Randy, age 7, said, "Be a good kisser. It'll make her forget that you never took out the trash."

WHAT WE ALL WANT

When a man and woman love each other and decide to marry, the last thing they think of during the marriage ceremony is "how can I grow indifferent and apathetic about my spouse." Unfortunately that's the direction the marriage turns. Gradually, the couple feels disconnected, and sometimes they turn on each other. One feels their needs aren't being met. Another may feel disrespected. They argue and fight over the smallest things and begin treating each other as enemies. Nobody marries with those intents in mind.

What causes this rift in marriages? And how do you avoid this dilemma so many marriages fall prey?

There are certain things to remember to ward off discouragement and disaster in the most important of human relationships. The Bible says in Genesis 2 that when people marry, it's the same as two people becoming one. When the 'you' and the 'I' become 'Us,' there's an immediate recipe for disaster if you're not careful. Why is that? When two people marry, they are uniting two different personalities, two different backgrounds, two different histories, two different sets of life standards and personal preferences, and two different egos. When married, they bring two different sets of perspective, expectations, dreams, and goals. The detonation fuse that can cause a marriage with potential to explode is selfishness. In the myriad of issues in a marriage there isn't just one spouse whose view is correct about everything, but selfishness makes one spouse think, *I'm right about this again. If only my spouse would listen to all my counsel, this marriage and our lives would run smoothly.*

What happens is that we take all the differences we have and hold them up against each other and one spouse thinks, *my experiences make me the better person to make the decisions.* The past histories and the different mindsets become tools of contention. We should view all the differences in life as experience we can use jointly to overcome obstacles and make well-defined decisions together. Instead of seeing our mindsets and personalities as barriers to happiness, we can understand how cleverly the Lord has used the experiences and personalities of each spouse to give them more tools and more weapons against the hardships of life and the enemy of their souls. When each spouse takes full advantage of their differences, they are more equipped than a couple where one domineers and makes all the decisions.

So how does a marriage survive and thrive in today's culture? The simple answer is that one self-centered person and the other self-centered person has to become 'Us.' This is the concept of "Us-ness." The Bible, in Genesis 2:24, says, "This explains why a man leaves his father and mother and is joined to his wife, and the two are united into one." "Us-ness" isn't two individuals fighting for their own rights and their own wants; it's two people making sacrifices and compromises for the sake of their relationship. In the end, the strength of the relationship supersedes the selfish desires of the individual of that relationship. But in any relationship, you don't just want it to survive, you want it to blossom. You don't want to just endure it; you want to enjoy it. Intimacy is the spice that adds exciting flavor to the marriage relationship.

The ingredients

Everyone has a desire for intimacy in their marriage, but many don't know how to achieve it. We are going to look at the four ingredients that create intimacy in your marriage. If you are mixing these four into the relationship on an ongoing basis, you stand a greater chance of having a deeper level of connectedness in the relationship. It develops the sense, "I'm feeling loved and I'm feeling cared about."

Intimacy is the strength of your relationship, and all four ingredients must be used. Compare this to making chocolate chip cookies. If we take out a big bowl and we pour the chips in, crack the eggs and drop them in, and neglect putting in the cookie mix, can you imagine what your cookie will taste like? You want a cookie, but instead you'll have chocolate chip scrambled eggs. That's not at all what you're after. What if you put in the mix, but no eggs or chips? You'd have a dry, tasteless end-product. To make a good chocolate chip cookie requires all the right ingredients. Intimacy is the same way. If you leave some things out, it won't be as great as you hoped. Dr. David Ferguson of Intimate Life Ministries identified four ingredients to intimacy.

Affectionate Caring

Affectionate caring communicates "I care about you." It's showing fondness, interest, concern, and attentiveness to your spouse.

If your wife is hurting, you express affectionate caring by saying something like, "I can see you're hurting. I just want you to know that I care. I'd love to listen."

Giving undivided attention when your spouse is talking also speaks affectionate caring. What do we typically do?

"Honey, can we talk?" she asks.

But you sit there watching TV, not wanting to turn it off, and not willing to look your spouse in the eye and communicate.

What predicts distress and divorce in relationships? It's the way you handle conflict through communication. Communication is the key component in any relationship, but the strongest factor in marriages. You're created to be more intimate and closer to your spouse than any other person throughout your life, thus the need to communicate takes the lead role. There is nothing more frustrating than marrying someone with the dream of living happily ever after, to find only a few years later that you're living in the house with someone who feels like a total stranger.

For example, if a wife finds joy in conversing with her husband and exploring into his daily life, but he simply comes home, plops in front of the television, eats his dinner, and goes to bed, while ignoring his wife's desire to verbally interact, she's going to feel uncared for. But what if you come home, share your day with her—not caring about turning on the tube and turning off your brain—and encourage her with love and affirmation? In the words of Gary Smalley in his book *Making Love Last Forever,* her love tank will be full. When her love tank is full, she will express heartfelt love back to you.

Another way of showing affectionate caring is prioritizing time for dating, talking, and affection. And if your spouse is dealing with something, promise to pray for them, actually do the praying, and then ask them later how things went. Too often we tell someone we'll do something and never get around to it. Why? It doesn't become a priority to us because we don't care enough.

For example, someone comes up to you in church, sharing a struggle or heartache, and then asks, "Will you pray for me?"

"Sure I will," you respond, but walk away and totally forget the whole thing. Honestly, we don't pray because we don't care.

Someone stopped me one Wednesday night and pulled me aside saying, "I want to share something with you. My wife's going into surgery this week. There are a couple cancerous masses they found. Would you pray for us?"

"Yes, I will" I said. "Right now."

Why did I pray with him right there instead of waiting until later? That was the need right then, and when you care, you meet that need. The heart of God is about caring, and so should ours.

Now what is the primary hindrance to affectionate caring? Anger and resentment. If you harbor anger and resentment in your heart toward your mate, how can you mix in the ingredient of affectionate caring? You can't care for someone if you're angry and resentful to them. So what's the remedy? You can't undo the past. You can't pretend the hurts, arguments, and misunderstanding never happened. Ephesians 4:31-32 spells out how to get affectionate caring back into the relationship: *Get rid of all bitterness, rage, anger, harsh words, and slander, as well as all types of malicious behavior. Instead, be kind to each other, tender-hearted, forgiving one another just as God through Christ has forgiven you.* Forgiveness is the choice you make to bring your ailing attitude back into a caring mode so you can choose to ardently love your spouse again.

Vulnerable Communication

Vulnerable communication to your mate says, "I trust you." It's about more than just talking about the weather or the news, it's about me being vulnerable enough to open up and share my thoughts, my fears, my hurts, and share my very being with my mate, believing I won't be put down, belittled, insulted, neglected, or criticized for how I feel. Trust is the foundation for any healthy relationship. Trust must also be present as you grow and mature spiritually. Each spouse must discern where the other may be struggling, and be ready to be sympathetic about the tough spiritual questions that arise when life can get hard or painful.

When it comes to trust, some of you might be thinking, "Oh, come on. We've been married now for eight years and I still can't get my spouse to open up and trust me."

The greatest hindrance to building trust is the emotion of fear. When you see a lack of trust, it's because there's some fear behind it. Fear of what? It could be fear of your reaction, fear of rejection, embarrassment, indifference, or humiliation. Fear keeps you from being vulnerable. Fear keeps you from sharing your heart. Why would I want to be vulnerable with you if I can't trust you? A couple may live with a pseudo sense of trust, which will lead to a pseudo sense of intimacy, which leaves you with only a pseudo sense of closeness. The reality is your marriage will never be strong or deep if you let fear dominate the relationship and your ability to vulnerably communicate. If you practice respect and vulnerable communication, your relationship will grow healthy and and fear is displaced with love and connection.

Why is fear such a problem? Fear takes away rational thought, steals your ability to love, and robs you of self-empowerment. 2 Timothy 1:7 says, "For God has not given us the spirit of fear, but of power, love, and self control." Whatever you fear ends up having power over you. Fear debilitates, but love empowers. Fear to be vulnerable with your spouse hinders intimacy.

So what do you do with fear? 1 John 4:18 says, "Such love has no fear because perfect love expels all fear."

Someone might ask, "What is perfect love?"

The first natural response would be to say, "God is perfect love." And that is true, but will just knowing God is perfect love make your fear go away? Having only an intellectual knowledge of God's love won't keep you from being scared. Simply having the mental ascent that the Lord loves you, He's in complete control, He watches over you and guards you against the enemy of your soul, and that He's given you thousands of promises that He'll never break will not expel your fear. It's only when you experience God's perfect love that fear's hold on you is ripped away. It's when you experience God's amazing love in your heart and soul by trusting Christ as your Lord and Savior that fear is driven out.

What this verse is saying is that it displaces fear. You can never totally cast out fear; it always has a way of creeping back in. The way to deal with fear is to come along side it and speak to it in love.

There is a wrong way of doing this. If a Christian brother is struggling with something and I realize there's fear there, I can say to him, "Oh, come on man. I know you're not afraid of that. There's really no big problem here. Just get over it!"

Is that going to take his fear away? Of course not.

I should say something like this: "Brother, I can see you're afraid. I just want you to know that I care, and I'm here for you to support you all the way, and we're going to make it together."

What do you think he would feel at the moment he hears those words? Speaking directly to his fear on some level is going to displace it, because now he doesn't feel like he's going through his issue alone.

Affectionate caring explodes any selfish motives for a spouse or a friend. When you acknowledge another's fear and stand by them, it shows you care. When you share an encouraging word, when you say that you love an individual and you're there to help ease the pain, you are communicating that you care. You may not be able to solve the problem for them but they will know they're not alone. People can endure almost anything if they know they're not alone and that someone cares about what they're going through.

Joint Accomplishment

Joint accomplishment has a unique dynamic in a relationship. It says, "I need you." Men relationally will build intimacy—a sense of connectedness—by doing things together. Joint accomplishment is displayed by doing specific tasks together, pursuing common interests, and setting and completing family goals. It could include things as simple as reading through the Bible and talking about how it's changing your life, working together to purchase some furniture, or saving money for a down payment on a house. What might be some things you'd want to do together?

It is through working together and accomplishing things together and finishing projects that you build a sense of intimacy.

You won't find a bunch of guys sitting around a table, just talking. "Well Bill, how many children do you have?" or "Do you think this tool belt makes me look fat?" Ladies are more inclined to talk about personal and family matters on the first meeting than guys. Men are talking about football, fishing, or fixing cars.

Let's say a couple of guys become friends and golfing buddies, they'll talk about anything trivial for a while, but over time they'll incorporate more of their personal life.

I had a golfing buddy, and we talked about everything under the sun, but after a couple of months he asked, "Rick, you've got kids, don't you?"

"Yeah."

"What are their ages?"

I began telling him, paused, and then started laughing.

"What's so funny?" he asked.

"Well, if we were a couple of ladies, we'd have known this on the first day. But as guys, it's taken us two months to get to that point."

Accomplishing things together builds intimacy, and it builds trust. It says to another that you're adding to my effort to make it faster or make it better. Sometimes it communicates that you've got gifts and talents that make our accomplishment much more successful than if I did it on my own.

The biggest hindrance to joint accomplishment is prideful self-reliance. This is the attitude that I can do this better than anyone else, so why let them come in here and mess it up. Even more harmful is the idea that no one else really cares so I'm not going to ask them because I don't want the rejection. I'll just struggle through it myself. What this says to others, even if you don't mean it to, is, "I don't need your care, I don't need your affection, I don't need you to tell me what to do, and I don't need your support."

Galatians 6:2 says, "Share each other's troubles and problems, and in this way obey the law of Christ." The word picture for troubles and problems is the image of a boulder. The reality about life is we'll all carry a boulder at some point—being divorced, facing a family death, or getting fired from a job. These are all big things in our life that will come down on us, but some might say, "I can handle it. I can do it myself. I don't need your support."

The Bible says that we do need to bear burdens together. When you're carrying that heavy load and it's bowing down your shoulders, it's my responsibility to come along side and place my shoulder under that weight and walk together with you, easing some of the pressure. Accomplishing things together creates intimacy that can't be done by two individuals working separately. The strongest relationships are forged when two carry the load of a tough time together. Why? It tells the other, "I'm with you. You're not alone."

Mutual Giving

Mutual giving means thinking more highly of your spouse than yourself. It's giving to your spouse instead of trying to get them to give to you. It's giving regardless of how they respond or how you feel. You choose the way you respond to others, and you decide how you're going to react and feel.

What are some ways I can do mutual giving?

You can initiate a 30 second phone call just to say, "I love you, and I'm looking forward to seeing you tonight." You can ask your spouse how you can help during a stressful time, and then do what is asked. Taking the kids can give your spouse time alone or with some friends. Helping your spouse complete unpleasant tasks is also showing mutual giving. But the most important aspect is to show what speaks love to spouse.

There are things you could do that aren't mutual giving.

Let's say you are conversing with your spouse and you say, "I know last week you gave to me, and you did all these wonderful things for me. Because you did that I gave back to you in the way you enjoyed most. But here's the problem dear: when I did those things, you didn't respond back in love."

Would expecting anything back in return be considered giving? No, it would be selfishness. If you're expecting a certain response or something given back, you didn't give; you're conducting a form of bartering. Basically you're saying, "I'll show you your kind of love, but I want you to show me my kind of love."

True giving happens when you do it just because you want to, regardless of the response.

The greatest example of giving without expecting a response is what the Lord Jesus Christ did for us. Jesus said that He came to save the perishing, to give hope to the hopeless, and to give us abundant life. His motive to give to us was not so that He would get something in return. There's nothing of any value we could give back to Him. From His love and compassion, Christ gave us what we needed simply because we so desperately needed it.

When Jesus said, "It is finished!" on the cross, He had extinguished God's wrath against our sin, defeated death, hell and the grave, and bought our freedom from the control of sin in our lives. It was a heavy price that cost Him his life. Jesus gave His life so all who believed would be forgiven.

But does He get bent out of shape because people don't respond? He doesn't say, "Look at those ingrates. I died for them to make them free, and they don't appreciate it and they don't like me." Does He complain and speak condescendingly toward mankind? No, He gave His best for us no matter how we respond. He didn't expect anything back. Our lack of response doesn't affect Him in any way. He gave because He loved us despite whether we loved Him back or not. Is He sad some people reject Him? Of course. He's got a heart of love and compassion. He sees the terrible hell where they're headed. He gave them a way of rescue, and they refused. As Dr. Herb Reavis, Jr. of North Jacksonville Baptist Church says, "Jesus is not a beggar. He's a King." He demonstrated His love for us by dying to rescue us. He rose again from the grave to give us life eternal.

Selfishness stymies mutual giving, so be on guard for it. Philippians 2:3-4 says, "Don't be selfish; don't live to make a good impression on others. Be humble, thinking of others as better than yourself. Don't think only about your own affairs, but be interested in others, too, and what they are doing." This is a difficult verse to live out because in reality all of us are selfish. I am selfish, controlling, and manipulative. I know these things about me. I don't like those facts about me, but I am that way. And there is a freedom in saying to you that I'm that way because it holds me accountable to God, myself, and others, so I can stop being that way. This keeps me humble and prevents me from thinking I'm better than anyone else. Without Christ directing my behavior, I'm no better off than any other man. With Christ's leading, I'm still not better than any other man, but I can live in a way that pleases Him and shows love to those around me.

* 15 *

CARESS YOUR RELATIONSHIP

Someone jokingly said, "You can live six weeks without food. You can live six days without water, but you can only live one day without toilet paper."

But seriously, every person—man, woman, boy, or girl—have certain intimacy needs in their life which they long to have met or they will be dwarfed or crippled in their emotional maturity. Have you ever met a grown-up whose immaturity and irresponsibility reminds you of an undisciplined teenager? Sometime in that person's life they hit a mental block where their emotional maturity level hit a brick wall. Somewhere along the way they had an experience or several experiences that emotionally shut them down. Somehow or some way their intimacy needs weren't met or they were discounted.

Everyone has intimacy needs. Those needs are anchored in relational response, rewards, or acknowledgement. People want to know they're wanted, loved, and appreciated by those they have the closest relationships with. Where you see the desire to have these intimacy needs met most are in parent-child relationships, spousal relationships, and to some degree, in friendships and work relationships.

So what are these intimacy needs? There are several core intimacy needs that people long to have fulfilled. I summarize these needs in the acronym CA⁶RESS, which is adapted from the work of Dr. David Ferguson of Intimate Life Ministries. The following list of core emotional needs was programmed into us at conception. Like food, air, water, and shelter, these emotional needs are biologically based. The difference is you cannot meet these needs on your own. They are met only in relationships.

Comfort

This need is met when you console, provide relief from stress, and offer peace and quiet enjoyment. It's to soothe, console, reassure, or respond to a hurting person with words, feelings, and touch. (Romans 12:15b; Matthew 5:4; 2 Corinthians 1:3-4; John 11:35)

Acceptance

This need is met through favorable reception. This is receiving and loving another person willingly and unconditionally, especially when the other's behavior has been imperfect. (Romans 5:7)

Attention

This need is met when those closest to you display consideration, courtesy and devotion. It's awareness, consciousness, and conveying appropriate interest, concern, and care, taking thought of another, and entering another's "world." (I Corinthians 12:25)

Affection

This need is supplied by exhibiting tender feelings toward another, and expressing care and closeness through physical touch. (Romans 16:16; Mark 10:16)

Appreciation

This need is met through an expression of gratitude. It's when thanks and praise are expressed for what another has accomplished or completed. (Colossians 3:15b; 1 Corinthians 11:2)

Affirmation

This need is met when reassuring a person for who they are and what they've accomplished, particularly when they're struggling with doubt. It's declaring something to be true thus making a positive statement or judgment. (2 Timothy 4:11).

Approval

This need is met when giving a favorable attitude or opinion about a person, their ideas, and their accomplishments. It's giving formal permission or sanction, building up or affirming another, and affirming both the fact and importance of another. A blessing. (Ephesians 4:29; Mark 1:11)

Respect

This need is met when you honor or esteem another, showing consideration or regard, responding to another with good will, or valuing someone highly. (Romans 12:10)

Encouragement

This need is met when you give courage, hope, or confidence consistently, but especially when they need it most, by urging another to persist and persevere toward a goal, or stimulating someone toward love and good deeds. (1 Thessalonians 5:11, Hebrews 10:24)

Support

This need is met when you encourage, shore up, or come alongside and gently help with a problem of another who's struggling or feeling overwhelmed. (Galatians 6:2)

Security

This need is met when you offer freedom from fear or threat of harm, providing relationship harmony and well-founded confidence. (Romans 12:16, 18)

All of us have those needs, and when they are met, we feel loved. When those needs aren't met, we feel a measure of pain, rejection, and invalidity. We are all born and created with these relational needs, and they never go away. If I grew up with my needs being ministered to, my life has great potential. If the needs aren't met, there is great pain.

Whether or not these relational needs are tended to, your emotions will be evoked, in a positive way when needs are attended or a negative way when they are ignored. From past and present experience, as well as past and present relationships, people contain inside them an "Emotional Cup." You can only "hold" so much emotion. Since emotional experiences are always being deposited, the cup will overflow, but what flows out is based on what has already filled the cup.

If your relational intimacy needs are met, the moods, the attitudes, and the words you say will brim with confidence, kindness, love, and understanding. When negative feedback is registered, it really has little effect because your "emotional cup" is already full of security and positive emotions. Sour emotions don't have any room in your cup.

Contrariwise, if your relational intimacy needs aren't met, your cup can fill up with bitterness, hurt, anger, anxiety, fear, and insecurities, and when you interact with others the responses you give are negative, pessimistic, and harmful. This overflows from what's inside you. The unfortunate reality is if others try to pour love and acceptance into your life after your cup's already been filled with rejection and hurt, those positive emotions have no room in your emotional cup. They drift away with the swelling spring of negative emotions continually pouring out of your cup.

It's easy to visualize what a person overflowing with positive emotions might look like, but the reality is we don't see that often. A person with a cup overflowing with pain and hurt is what we most often encounter. The important question is if my cup is filled with hurting and unhealthy emotions, how do I empty out the bad stuff so I can begin filling it with the positive emotions?

This is what the emotional cup could hold:

Stress

Anxiety

Fear…insecurities

False Guilt

True Guilt, often from retaliation

Bitterness—Resentment—Hurt—Anger

Here are some of the symptoms of an emotional cup filled with an accumulation of unhealthy emotion:

Sleep/Appetite Disturbance

Loss of Energy and Concentration

The "escape" into things like Work, Drugs, Infidelity, Pornography, etc.
Depression
Impatience and a quick temper
Physical side effects that lead to health issues
Loss of Positive Emotions like Joy, Love, Affection, Romance

In order to empty the unhealthy accumulation of emotions, first they must be acknowledged and identified. A solution can never be created until the problem is revealed. Ask yourself these diagnostic questions:

Hurt—In what ways and in what relationships have I felt "wounded" with words or actions?
Anger—Who do I avoid, reject, criticize, or otherwise retaliate against?
Bitterness/Resentment—Who do I wish harm on? Talk evil of? Or strive to not be like?
True Guilt—What have I done that would hurt, reject, wrong, wound, or otherwise show contempt or disrespect?

Each issue must be dealt with thoroughly and relentlessly. Storing negative emotions will suck the life right out of you. When those poisonous emotions are evicted, your soul will experience a sense of freedom that will make each day and the future ahead seem brighter.

So what do intimacy needs look like in average everyday life? I'll show you. Let's say I'm a five years old who has these needs for attention, affection, appreciation, comfort, support, security, respect, encouragement and approval. (At five, I don't know I have these needs, but that doesn't make them any less real.) We'll go a step further and say these needs are being met. Here is an example of a moment in a five year old's life.

"Hi Dad," I say as he walks through the door after working all day. "Look Daddy! Look! I've been drawing this picture of me and you, and we got this big, huge fish! We were fishing all day and look what we caught."

"Let me see that," Dad says, taking the picture from my hands and examining it. "Now tell me about this again."

"Well see, Daddy. It's a picture of you and me, and we got this giant new fishing pole and we got this big fish with it, and the fish was 500 pounds."

"Whoa! That's a picture of you and me. Man, I bet we had fun! You know what? I am so thankful for you. I'm going to put this on the refrigerator."

That memory stays in that five year old's mind. When Dad stops and invests interest, kind words, and time into his son, he is meeting the subconscious needs of the boy: attention and appreciation.

If this happens on a consistent basis, the boy begins to develop in a positive fashion, having positive emotions deposited into him. As he grows, his underlying foundational thought will be, "I must be important." That's not pride. We all want to feel important. We all want to feel like what we're doing means something. This gives the boy the drive to not be discouraged, but to keep striving for more good things. The consistent deposits will shore him up if a challenge comes his way as he matures. "Dad loves me. He thinks I'm important. He believes in me. I can do this!"

If you've got little children and you give them positive reinforcement, what are they going to do? They'll draw you one picture after another after another. You might think this is cute or funny, but keep ministering to the need because the need is there and when you do they feel loved. When you meet the need they respond in positive ways. The way you respond to your kids in love reflects to them how God will respond to them. If they're saying to themselves, "My father loves me for who I am," when they're confronted with the Lord, they can easily think, "My Heavenly Father loves me." When they repent of their sin and believe in Christ as Savior, they won't feel God's threatening, strict, or indifferent. The way children see their fathers is the way they see God. If you've messed up as a father or been absent, the Lord can still make His true character known. I thought God was a drill sergeant when the Lord first saved me, and I served Him out of fear, because I viewed God through the lenses of who my father was. As I've grown in my relationship with God, I serve Him out of thankfulness and love, but I still have a healthy sense of fear of Him because He is mighty and in control.

When you meet your child's intimacy needs, they will think positively. They will then feel loved and cared for. They will develop a sense of security, and they will feel grateful. When we meet those needs—needs that all people intrinsically have—then you will find it leads to productive behaviors. They will be kind. They will be giving and considerate. They'll pursue excellence. Why? They are going to keep developing themselves in a positive way because the environment you create says "you can do it." The outcome is a healthy family, they gain healthy caring relationships, their character and personality matures, and they grow in faith. All this takes place because starting way back in their childhood you consistently took time to minister to their intimacy needs.

All of that sounds wonderful, but let's see what it looks like when we see the converse of this. We'll take the same five year old with the same needs.

Dad comes home from work, plops down in the recliner and turns on the news.

I come over with my picture and say, "Daddy, I'm so glad you're home. I've been working on this picture all day. See? It's a picture of me and you, and we got this new fishing pole, and caught this giant fish!"

"Son, can't you see I'm watching the news?" Dad says.

"Well, yes sir. But Daddy, look. I drew this picture of me and you fishing, and we caught this huge fish. It was 500 pounds!"

"Son, I told you I'm watching the news. You're being real inconsiderate. Don't you think?"

"But Daddy, I got this picture…"

"Son, get out of the room," Dad interrupts. "You're bothering me. I can't hear the news."

That just sent a message to the boy. "Son, I don't want to see your picture. It doesn't matter to me." That in turn is translated in the boy's mind as "I don't matter to him." His needs for attention and appreciation were not met. The response the boy received—even if it wasn't meant as such—is what was important to him, but he left feeling ignored, disapproved, rejected, and criticized.

When that need isn't met you can begin to think in one of two different ways. Whenever a challenge or a difficulty occurs in your life, you have a foundational thinking pattern that says "I guess I can't do this. There must be something wrong with me." You quit trying. Tragically, when this happens, people turn to alcohol or drugs. They become character-disordered people. They are angry. They are manipulative. They are controlling.

In many families, because of a harsh and neglectful upbringing some of those children grow up as adults and quite trying. They give up and let life pass by them. These may have multiple marriages, struggle with depression, and maybe even find problems holding a job. Because of the neglect of the CA⁶RESS needs being met in their life and the sense that they don't matter, they believe this false message and quit trying.

Some don't give up. Some just keep trying harder.

"Daddy, you don't like the picture? It really wasn't that good anyway. And yeah, I forgot you don't like to fish. I know you're a Marine. So Daddy, how about this: I got a tank. I drew a tank, and it's a tank like back when you were in the Marine Corps. Don't you like Marines?"

"Son, you don't get it, do you? I don't care about that stupid picture. I'm working right now."

"Okay, Daddy, you're right. It is a stupid picture. I don't like Marines either. Let me see what else I can do. Oh yeah! I know. How about this…"

What happens is you keep trying harder and harder and harder, and you become an overachiever. Why? By trying harder these overachievers are trying to get someone to say that they care. They're still trying to get their intimacy needs met. Even though you won't admit it if you are an overachiever, you harbor a lot of hurt, anger, fear, shame, and condemnation. And when you carry unhealthy thinking with the unhealthy feelings that go with it, here's what happens: you become a perfectionist or you start acting out in things like addictions, pornography, or manipulative behavior. You begin playing controlling games with people to get them to do what you want. You become a liar, deceiving even those closest to you. A destructive habit also emerges where you take on addictive behaviors, forms of rebellion, personality disorders, and poor character. Insecurity and immaturity mark your life. Strangely, all this occurs because somewhere back in your family somebody didn't care.

Intimacy needs in marriage

I submit to you that the good and bad consequences also happen in a marriage depending on whether intimacy needs are met. Just as for children, the closest relationship they have is with their parents, so in marriage, the most intimate relationship you have is with your spouse.

When each partner comes into a marriage, there is the usual expectation of giving and receiving. The presumption is your spouse will fulfill the needs you have of affection, appreciation, approval, comfort, and security. Both spouses should seek to do this for the other, but the problems develop when expectation meets with disappointment. Too often, one spouse begins to think the other is obligated to meet their emotional needs almost like a slave, and when it doesn't happen, tension and bitterness builds and leads to conflict.

Why does this happen? Maybe they never had their intimacy needs met growing up, and they placed their expectations on this new, close relationship to fulfill their emotional longings. The thought is that your spouse will know what you need and dedicate their life to making you happy and whole. Unfortunately when one spouse has great expectations and the other has no clue about them, the ingredients for frustration are about to be stirred together.

Everybody has intimacy needs. We can say it's unfair to one spouse to have such prospects placed upon them, but in one way or another we all do it. So what's the answer? Love your spouse. That sounds simple, and it doesn't mean to simply show emotional feelings toward them. It means to be a student of your spouse. What do they need? What do they like? What do they enjoy? Your spouse should be your biggest hobby, so learn as much about them as you can so you can meet their needs, but be sure to communicate. The natural response of a spouse whose needs are met is to reciprocate, but often times they don't know how. Communication keeps them informed about what you like so when they're overflowing with love they can meet your needs.

It's not your responsibility to make your spouse love you the way you want. Be faithful in doing your part to make your partner feel loved. They will understand your love and devotion, and they will dedicate themselves to nurturing you. If you choose not to address the intimacy needs, there will be great pain from the one you've chosen to spend the rest of your life with. Since your spouse is who you spend the majority of your time and energy on, why not invest in making a great relationship instead of a miserable one? Ultimately, you'll be the one to look back in shame and realize, "I saw she needed comfort and I didn't care." Is it any wonder she thinks there's something wrong with her? Is there any doubt why she thinks you don't care? If you invest the time to meet the need, she will think you love her.

Is it any wonder we have more character-disordered men and woman today? Starting back in their childhood and onward, they've been given this message: I don't care about your needs for attention, appreciation, approval, acceptance, affirmation, respect, and comfort. I don't care. Unfortunately, as we grow up, those needs don't go away. So what do some people do? They find a way to meet those needs themselves through things like drugs, alcohol, or pornography in order to deaden the pain from the unmet need. That really doesn't help. The need is still going unmet.

The only way comfort can be administered is when someone says, "I can see you're hurting, and I want you to know I care." I speak to the pain and comfort the pain.

"That must have been tough on you, and I'm sorry that happened." I come along side and empathize, letting them know they're not alone.

"That must have been really scary for you to have that happen, and I want you to know that I'm here to support you even while you're going through this." This will decrease the amount of fear and build a sense of connectedness so they won't feel like they're in this all alone.

"But what if I'm the one who needs the encouragement?" you may ask. I would suggest you seek comfort first from the Lord and His Word. He's never fickle. He's completely compassionate. And He's the only one who can bring true healing to your hurting soul.

Then I would plant seeds of encouragement in others' lives so that you, too, will begin to reap a harvest of encouragement. The interesting thing about this principle about sowing into another to reap benefits for yourself is that the real healing takes place when you comfort someone else instead of waiting to be comforted yourself. The reason is you take your eyes off yourself and you send your energy on helping others, which is what the Lord designed you for in order to be emotionally healthy. Helping others brings healing in your own heart as well as in the lives of others. This is true for parenting. This is true for marriages. This is true for your church relationships.

* 16 *

NAKED AND NOT ASHAMED—SEX AND MARRIAGE

What are the two most important issues in marriage? Sex and money. How do we know this? Research shows sexual problems are the #2 reason for divorce in America. The #1 issue is money problems. These problems are prominent even in Christian couples. The real question is whether it's the problems that cause divorce or is there a greater dynamic involved? In an earlier chapter we addressed what predicts distress and divorce, and understood how couples resolve conflict determines their success rate. Even though money and sex are the two big topic areas people fight about, what predicts distress and divorce is the degree of willingness to communicate and solve problems.

Sexual issues used to be misunderstood because nobody talked about them. Today, sex is practiced so recklessly and recreationally that the experience has lost its wonder. The Lord intended sex to be a special gift reserved exclusively for a husband and wife who've committed to be with each other for a lifetime. In the modern sexual revolution, sex has no boundaries, and involves no commitments. Love is no longer a prerequisite for sex; in fact, some have intercourse with people they might not necessarily like.

The irony of it is those perverting God's gift of sex appears to be enjoying it the most, while those who've committed to each other seems to have lost the joy and excitement of the experience. The Lord intended sex to be thrilling and fulfilling. Whether we grasp that fact or not, He is the designer of it, and He sets the limitations on it for our own good.

So what does it mean to enjoy sex in the safety of marriage? How do we get over the misunderstandings that say sex is bad and has to be endured instead of embraced? And what are some ways we can refuel the passion in our physical intimacy?

We're going to talk about what God meant for sex, and what He intended it to be. There are some great resources that talk about the physical and behavioral aspects of sex with your spouse, a couple of them being Tim Lahaye's *The Act of Marriage* and Dr. Doug Rosen's *Celebrating Sex*. What we're going to concentrate on are the needs for sex and the different types of sex we actually can experience.

What was God's intent for sex? Some may say He created it for procreation, and that's true, because without it we couldn't have babies. Others may say God created sex for emotional bonding between a husband and wife, which is also correct. Sex is the most intimate and vulnerable people can get. You can't get any closer together physically than during the act of sex. Human sex is such a beautiful gift from God, because of the excitement, of course, but most interestingly because no other creation on this earth but a man and a woman practice sex face-to-face. What else was God's intent for sex? It's an action, a behavior. He gave sex to us as the ultimate physical experience.

Sexual guilt

Sex is meant for enjoyment, but many feel guilt where sex is involved. With today's promiscuity, sex has become cheap and meaningless. As a doctor who has practiced for many years, I can tell you I've never met a couple, especially if they're Christian, that has had premarital sex and not experienced guilt. Those couples who experience premarital intercourse consistently report lower marital satisfaction over the years. I would ask this, "What will be different on your honeymoon?" The answer is nothing, because the excitement and expectation of first time intercourse is cheapened by premarital sex. What is the honeymoon meant for? It's meant to experience intercourse and sexual union between two people. When you've experienced sex prior to marriage and you have that wonderful orgasm on your honeymoon, how do you feel inside? From women the typical response is guilt. Do you think God intended you to suffer guilt after such a wonderful physical experience? The answer is no. Who is hurting whom? You hurt yourself. For guys who don't save sex for marriage as God planned, when they get to it on their honeymoon, there's nothing special. It's just the same old thing.

But there is great news. The Lord can take the pain and the guilt when you repent and revive your love and commitment, making it fresh and new. God loves resurrecting things. I always believe that if a couple will make a decision to stop premarital intercourse and wait until their marriage, then the honeymoon will be much more enjoyable and meaningful because you'll be doing what God wanted.

Different types of sex

Sex is a celebration. It's more than a physical experience; it's an action that you can engage all your sense in: physical, mental, and emotional. Sex can also be therapeutic. It can be for fun, or it can be a springboard to regain a sense of intimacy. There are different types of sex, and we're going to look at them in a fun way.

Orange Juice Sex

One type of sex you'll experience is what I call "orange juice" sex. You might think, "What is orange juice sex?" Well, what is orange juice? It's something filled with vitamins that's good for your body and health. Orange juice sex is that good sexual experience that energizing to your body and soul, and brings a lot of health to the relationship.

Ice Cream Sex

Ice cream sex is very different than orange juice sex because it's all about pure fun. It's like 31 flavors and you can try all you can. Grab two spoons, dig right in, and eat all the ice cream you want.

Sneaker Sex

Do you have a pair of old shoes you just can't get rid of because they're so comfortable? Sneaker sex is like that. There aren't a lot of bells and whistles to it. It just feels comfortable. It's not all fun like ice cream, and it's not all healthy for you like orange juice; it just feels right.

Yoke Sex

Now what is a yoke? It's a collar used primarily for two oxen pulling a plow. Do they want to be there? Not necessarily. In the same fashion, you'll have yoke sex. For one reason or another you don't want to be there, but you'll do it anyway. Do you know why? It's because you're a team, and you're yoked together. Sometimes you might get annoyed because it's not ice cream sex, but it can't always be ice cream. That's not reality. Now if you have "yoke" all the time, that's not healthy. Sometimes, it's going to be different. Enjoy the variety.

Procreation Sex

Procreation sex is not about ice cream, and it's not orange juice. It's deliberate and intentional.

The wife will say, "Okay honey, it's 12:02 am, the moon is just right, and I've positioned my body at the right angle. It's time."

What's the goal of procreation sex? It's to have intercourse when she is most fertile so she can get pregnant. This kind of sex is intended for making families.

Cathedral Sex

When you go to church and experience the Lord's peace and presence, and you sense your mind, spirit, and body are one with God, there's this feeling like everything is right in the world. It's a spiritual, harmonious episode that sends you into heavenly bliss. There are times in our lives when all is right with our relationship, when we're unshaken by what's going on around us, and enjoy sex for the fun, bonding, and simple enjoyment of it. Ladies tend to favor this kind. Men are more interested in the ice cream or orange juice. It will be different, so be thankful.

A word of caution

If you're always expecting ice cream, you'll be disappointed because it won't always be that way. Sex will be become a contentious subject if you always demand your way. What happens in marriages, Christian and non-Christian, is one desires sex in only a particular way while the other prefers something different. You may have a preference, but fatigue, a bad day at work, or dealing with rude attitudes may not make your spouse feel as fun and spunky as you. Occasionally, it'll be yoke sex. Sometimes it's orange juice or ice cream. Whatever the case, be thankful for the time together—but especially be thankful for your spouse.

The greatest enjoyment in the act of sex is having the goal of satisfying and exciting your mate, not just yourself. When you concentrate on your spouse's pleasure, don't worry, you won't be left out. The experience will be reciprocal. Listen to what the Apostle Paul says in 1 Corinthians 7:2-4:

But since there is so much immorality each man should have his own wife and each woman her own husband. The husband should not deprive his wife of sexual intimacy, which is her right as a married woman, nor should the wife deprive her husband. The wife gives authority over her body to her husband, and the husband also gives authority over his body to his wife.

Someone might ask, "What do you mean, I have no right to my body? He can do whatever he wants? Is that what it's says?"

That's not what that verse is implying. It simply means that a wife's body doesn't belong to her alone. It doesn't say you don't have a right to what happens to your body, because it indicates you do. It's just not yours alone, but also your husband's. In the same way, the husband's body doesn't belong to him alone, but also to his wife.

Don't deprive each other except by mutual consent and for a time so you may devote yourselves to prayer. Wife, you can't give your husband the excuse: "Well, honey, I know it's been a month, but I'm still in prayer and fasting." This is wrong. Paul tells us the dangers of this in 1 Corinthians 7:5:

So do not deprive each other of sexual relations. The only exception to this rule would be the agreement of both husband and wife to refrain from sexual intimacy for a limited time, so they can give themselves more completely to prayer. Afterward they should come together again so that Satan won't be able to tempt them because of their lack of self-control.

It is acknowledged in the Bible that mankind has a problem concerning sexual self-control. In fact, when you see a list of sins mentioned in scripture, typically, you will always see the sexual sins mentioned first. They are the predominant ones. Imagine that if back in the early church days, Paul was reciting a list of sins beginning with immorality and fornication before he moves to greed, anger, and the like, that they had the same struggles in his day as we do in ours. The difference is now it's much more pervasive and readily accessible. All you have to do is click on a mouse, and there it is.

As we consider these verses from 1 Corinthians 7:2-5, there are four principles we must think about.

Both husband and wife have sexual needs and drives that should be fulfilled

Both have sexual needs and drives that should be fulfilled only in marriage. Sadly, we're in a culture that basically says, "I can get my sexual needs met without being married if I want to, or even if I am married I can get creative with different ways outside my marriage to be satisfied."

We have couples nowadays who consider themselves as "Swingers." This is when a husband and wife go to swinging clubs, meet up with another couple, and have sex by swapping out spouses. It's all with mutual consent for those involved. But this is not what God intended marriage to be like. It's a distortion, a perversion. When God made Adam and Eve, He saw the completeness of their relationship and said it was "very good." God's creation was wholesome and right. Adam and Eve were naked and not ashamed. Satan tries to take anything God makes and distort it. As we look around we see the sex issue—which was a gift from God—is distorted in our world.

The first principle is both husband and wife have sexual needs and drives that should be fulfilled in marriage. From early adolescence, males have a natural drive to express themselves sexually. But as a redeemed churchgoer, I somehow got the notion women typically didn't like it or want it. When taking a human sexuality course at seminary, myself, two other guys, and two ladies were sitting at a table in the student center talking about what we'd learned. I'll never forget the interchange.

"Where do you guys get off thinking you're the only ones who want sex?" one of the ladies asked. "I want it, too!"

"You do?" I asked. "I thought females never wanted it."

"No. I have those feelings, too." She coached me on a woman's experience. Biologically, men and women are different, but women do enjoy sex and have sexual needs.

Individuals forfeit control of their body to their spouse

Many guys are saying, "I'm all yours, baby!"

Some women are thinking, "I don't want to give that brute unrestricted access to do whatever he wants."

As we consider this principle, we must clarify that your spouse doesn't have the right to control you nor abuse you. No spouse has the right to do whatever they want to their partner.

One thing I'll never forget is when my human sexuality professor said, "The Bible doesn't prescribe what you do in bed, but it *proscribes* who you do it with." Look at that phrase again. The whole point was the Bible is silent about what you do in the bedroom, but it's explicit about you having sexual relations with your spouse.

"That's a broad statement," I said.

Professor Dow turned to me, and I jokingly added, "In that case, I'll use whips and chains tonight."

"No," he rebutted, knowing my playful character. "There are other principles in the scripture that always apply. Whatever you do with your spouse must fortify and edify the marriage. It should never demean or tear down the other person. It should always respect their views, their wishes, and their wants."

If you desire to do something, but it's a turnoff to your spouse, your thoughts should turn to a decision to be either selfish or esteem your spouse's wishes more highly than your own. The selfish option may give you pleasure for a moment, but it will plant seeds of contention and bitterness for a long time. If you love your spouse and respect their wish, chances are they'll be willing to later respect your longings. Esteeming your spouse exemplifies the "us-ness" philosophy where neither of us is in it for selfish agendas, but instead to create a powerful, enjoyable union as husband and wife.

When a spouse forfeits control of their body to their spouse, it's in the atmosphere and attitude that your spouse is loving and means to give you pleasure according to how you define it. Forfeiting control of your bodies to each other enables both spouses to enjoy the pleasure and fulfillment of bonding in a physical act.

Both partners are forbidden to refuse meeting their mate's sexual needs

This issue comes up increasingly more in counseling through the years. It causes such tension in a relationship, it eventually forces one of the partners to snap and give up on the entire marriage.

I have counseled a woman in a downward-spiraling marriage who withheld sex from her husband for two years. She had caught him having an affair a couple years back. He forsook his mistress, repented, tried earnestly to make up for his sin against her, but she was hurt badly by the betrayal and cut herself off from him.

"You aren't responsible for his choice to have an affair," I told her. "But you must accept responsibility for the weakening of the relationship. Since he's repented to you and God and has dramatically changed his ways, you have the power to forgive. Withholding is weakening your relationship."

On the flip-side of the coin, men, if you're not acting out your role as a servant-leader, and if you don't make your wife feel loved, cherished, and respected, don't you think she'll find it hard to be physically intimate and close with you?

What makes you think you can jump into bed with her and have your way when in her heart is anger and resentment which you have caused.

Reflect on what's important to your spouse, not just what you desire.

The most important aspects of physical lovemaking are communication and a healthy relationship. Understand what each enjoys and hopes for and build a unity in your marriage that is trustworthy and solid.

Marriage is approved by God

This last principle is self-explanatory. The act of heterosexual marriage is approved and blessed by God.

SEXUAL DIFFERENCES BETWEEN MEN AND WOMEN

Difference in attitudes

Sex is about the physical experience for men. For women, it's relational.

For Men

Men were created with a physical drive to release their passions in a way that women were not. We'll go more in depth soon, but generally men have the overwhelming desire for sex caused by the daily multiplication of sperm that must be released. But make no mistake: men aren't just simple sex-crazed maniacs. The brains of men are compartmentalized in such a way that they can pour all their passion and energy into whatever they're thinking about. Men are wired to be more single-minded than women. If they're involved in a sport, all their willpower, strength, and emotions go into that activity. When they see their wife, their attitude is basically to get excited and aroused. When a man pours his energy into the physical desire for his wife, no distractions can take his mind from her. Somebody could be pounding on his door, but his focus is on her. I think this may be misunderstood by many women as "he only wants sex." If the husband loves his wife and makes her feel loved, it's actually a great compliment which says, "I only want you. This is my greatest way of showing it."

The compartmentalization can sometimes be unhealthy. Because of a man's focus on his sexual relationship with his wife, he can be angry and resentful toward her, but still have a great sexual experience. But when men have their orgasm is when they are most vulnerable emotionally.

For Women

The woman is more emotionally vulnerable before the act of marriage. When married, the attitude of sex is relational. Where men can become more compartmentalized and focused, women see the sexual experience as holistic. She wants to know that the relationship is healthy, growing, and that there's a deep sense of "Us-ness" and connectedness. A woman's attitude about sex affects her total being. That explains why a wife can't enjoy the act when she's at odds with her husband. She doesn't need any physical release like her husband does. When she enjoys sex is when she feels loved. Don't overlook that last sentence. It's the key to a happy, enjoyable sex life. It's not about if she knows she's loved. She may know she's loved without feeling it. For the wife, each day desires to have her love nurtured. She wants to hear that you love her. She wants to feel—in a nonsexual way—that you love her, and she wants to experience that she's loved through appreciation, thanks, and adoration. Her sexual drive doesn't come from physical stimulation, but through meeting emotional needs. Will it take hard work for you to study your wife and discover what meets her needs? It will, because it'll build a bond between you that will surpass even the sexual experience.

Differences in stimulation

For men, it is body-centered. Men focus almost exclusively on what they see. The world of television, billboards, and especially pornography reinforces the issue of sight. Men can tend to be focused on the technique or the position. Fragrance and behavior are also factors in stimulation.

For women this is not so. She is person-centered. She doesn't concentrate on the act of sex. She is focused on the relationship and on her husband. Her consideration could be, "How are you doing as my husband?" "How are you doing in loving me?" "How are you doing as my life mate?" She is also centered on touch. She doesn't want sex that will cause discomfort or pain. Where men may want to be aggressive; ladies want to be more sensual and slow so they can savor the moment.

Here's a word of warning to prevent poisoning the act of sex and the attitude each spouse will have toward it. There is a difference between fantasy and reality. If you view pornography, you sabotage the joy of sex. How? If you look at pornography, you will hear very aggressive talk, a lot of filth, and if you watch it long enough, you subconsciously will try to recreate it in your bedroom. When you do that, you're not making love to your spouse. You are selfishly trying to live out the vision planted in your mind. Fantasy and reality will never match. As long as you try to recreate what you've seen using your spouse, you'll never reach reality, and you will always be disappointed. Is it your spouse's problem? No, it's yours. You must end what is distorting your reality, and forsake the pornography sights.

Differences in needs

Men need respect. Women desire love.

God lays down these guidelines to happiness in marriage, and He gives different directives to each spouse. In Ephesians 5:21-26, the Bible says, "And further, you will submit to one another out of reverence for Christ. You wives will submit to your husbands as you do to the Lord…And you husbands must love your wives with the same love Christ showed the church. He gave up His life for her to make her holy and clean."

The word 'submit' could easily be replaced with the word "respect." The scripture exhorts each spouse to respect one another, but it goes further by explaining how to meet the most important needs of each spouse. For the husband, it's respect. For the wife, love is paramount.

With that knowledge, we have the choice to meet our spouse's needs or not. If you want only your needs met but won't provide what your spouse yearns for, you are sabotaging the relationship you forsook all others for. When you married your spouse you decided everybody else is canceled off your list. Ephesians 5:31 says, "For this cause shall a man leave father and mother, and shall join with his wife, and the two shall be one flesh." When you neglect your spouse's needs, you are hurting yourself. No one gets married to inherit an enemy that'll oppose them for the rest of their lives. But if we're not careful, our wedding vows to "love each other through better or worse and through richer or poorer" can turn into "I don't like you and I hate you all the more." If you desire to be happy with the person you've committed to spend the rest of your life with selfishness goes out the window. The greatest way for you to find satisfaction in your marriage is to bring satisfaction to your spouse.

The culture tells us otherwise, saying, "If you want satisfaction, you've got to do what feels good."

Christ, however, gave us an example to follow: if you love your spouse, sacrifice yourself to provide what they need.

But you may ask, "If I spend my life energy meeting my spouse's needs, when are mine going to be met?" That's the great paradox this self-absorbed culture doesn't seem to grasp. First, if you are focused on being a blessing to your spouse, you won't be saturated in self-centered thinking, which is natural to all humans. But when you meet your spouse's needs, it's like planting seeds. The seeds you plant may not sprout immediately, but as long as you tend them they'll eventually produce a great harvest. In other words, when you focus on meeting your spouse's needs, your spouse will be very interested in meeting yours. As a wise old deacon once said, "Concentrate on loving and blessing your spouse, expecting nothing in return, and what you'll get back will be far more than you could ever have wanted."

Men, when you fulfill the role of a servant leader, a wife will be more inclined to trust your judgments and respect you as head of the home. As a wife respects, a husband will love. Men find it difficult to love when they're not being respected.

When the husband consciously makes sure the needs are met at home—placing the marriage and the relationship above work and career—the wife will desire to meet his needs.

There is a great word of caution I want to expend. Because each person has a selfish, sinful nature, there is the potential to totally violate all the good intentions meant in marriage. This built-in contention goes all the way back to man's fall into sin recorded in Genesis 3. The curse of sin spelled out underlying agendas in each gender. Wives will want to control their husbands. Husbands will want to be the masters of their wives. The only thing that can counteract that sinful desire is the example of Christ to love and respect, and the only way we are empowered to overcome our sin is through the leadership of the Holy Spirit guiding our lives.

Differences in orgasms

For men, orgasms are shorter, more intense, and more physically oriented. Your husband is looking at your curves and at your body; he's stimulated by sight.

For women, it's longer, more in depth, and it's holistic, meaning it's about the whole experience, not just the physical aspect. Are you being respectful? Have you met her emotional and relational needs ahead of time? Does she feel that you are a part of the household events and are cooperative with the kids? All of that will invest into her willingness to give herself over sexually.

Here's a mistake women make. Many say, "All he cares about is getting what he wants." There's some truth in that, because men are physical and not easily distracted. It is impossible for a woman to empathize with a husband about his sexual needs because his is completely different than hers. A woman has absolutely no physical need for release through orgasm. A man is created to experience the physical release that comes through sex.

Men also make a grave mistake. Once a husband knows all is well at home, his sexual needs are met, and he has three square meals a day, he may tend to put his attention elsewhere. He may start enhancing his career or get involved in a sport or hobby, and begin neglecting what his wife enjoyed the most—spending quality time with her. A woman longs for her husband to share the inner workings of his life, his dreams, his goals, and his love for her. It means the world to her if she knows you care. If she knows you can sympathize with her anxieties without trying to solve the problem, if she knows you'll be there for her no matter what, and if you perform the role of servant leadership, she feels loved and adored. A wife has the innate desire to feel secure in her relationship and in her life with her husband.

Once we understand we have different needs, we can understand each other better. Sometimes it can seem like learning a different language but the time and effort you spend on it will be well invested. A great sex life in marriage goes far beyond just the physical act. It encompasses love, respect, and meeting everyday practical needs. The act of sex is never the main course; it's more like a fine dessert at the end of a healthy meal.

* 17 *

WHAT HE WANTS. WHAT SHE WANTS.

The greatest enjoyment, but also the source of the greatest friction, in the marriage relationship is lovemaking. Now why am I going to discuss this just in the arena of marriage? After all, don't unmarried people also make love? Upfront, let's clear this matter. Unmarried people only have sex. Lovemaking comes from people who are in love. Love entails responsibility, sacrifice, and selflessness. If one person truly loves another, they will share the act of lovemaking in the safety of marriage as God designed it. This may not be politically correct, but who cares. It's right. Too much research shows the dangers, troubles, and emotional scarring that occurs with being sexually active outside of being married.

Unfortunately, sexual friction in marriage is a huge problem. When we think about the two most defining factors that lead to divorce, we see money problems as number one. The number two reason for divorce is—you guessed it—sexual issues.

I believe sexual issues in marriage are caused by lack of communication, lack of understanding, and recycled stereotypes. Many wives have heard and now believe this line: "Well, all he cares about is strictly having his needs met and that's all sex is about." In a physiological and biological sense that may be true, but don't negate, ladies, that men are also emotional beings even though they try to act like they aren't.

Many husbands think wives have absolutely no interest in the sexual aspect and that wives like to use sex only as a weapon by depriving their husbands of it. From what I've learned from the comments of female students, ladies do actually enjoy the act of sex, but they like the process of getting to the bedroom as much as the act itself. They like to be romanced and they want to feel beautiful.

Knowledge is power. We're going to bypass the myths and biases about sex and discuss why it's significant to the man and what it means to the woman. Think about it. If the Lord made this the pinnacle experience for a married couple, why aren't more enjoying this gift? After all, sex is the physical expression of our emotional love and commitment to each other. In this chapter we're going to learn five reasons lovemaking is significant to your husband, and we'll look at what lovemaking means to the wife. The following is from the book *The Five Sex Needs of Men and Women* by Gary and Barbara Rosberg.

The top five reasons for the husband are:
1. It satisfies his sex drive.
2. It fulfills his manhood.
3. It enhances his love for his wife.
4. It reduces friction in the home.
5. It provides life's most exciting experience.

Here are the top five things it means to the wife:
1. It fulfills her womanhood.
2. It reassures her of her husband's love.
3. It satisfies her sex drive.
4. It relaxes her nervous system.
5. It provides the ultimate experience for her, as well.

Instead of developing all five of the husband's points followed by the wife's, I thought it would be interesting to see them concurrently. There are two purposes behind this. First, you won't be able to get involved in the one that interests you and neglect the other. Second, you can see how the whole complex design of relationship and marriage works from both sides so you can develop understanding and a growing sense of intimacy.

1. It satisfies his sex drive

God designed man to be the aggressor, provider, and leader of his family. Somehow that's tied to his sex drive. The woman who resents her husband's sex drive while enjoying his aggressive leadership needs to face the fact she can't have one without the other.

It's a reality that men are visually stimulated. They're much more visually stimulated than women are. Men are also different than women biologically. Unlike women, men have a physical need for sexual expression.

Caution: what we're about to talk about is for mature minds only.

Why do men have this physical need? Every drop of semen fluid contains as many as 300 million sperm. A man can have two to five ejaculations a day, depending upon his age, thus a man's reproductive system manufactures and supplies many millions of tiny sperm daily. If unreleased through coitus (coitus is just a technical term for intercourse), this becomes frustrating to his mental and physical well-being. Semen builds up every 48 to 72 hours and needs to be released. Even at the biological level, can you see what sexual tension builds in men?

If a guy goes around without sex two weeks, four weeks, two months, four months, and you're using sex as a weapon, understand you are creating, even at the biological level, a lot of sexual frustration because the body wants to release it. On the other hand, husbands can't be saying, "Well, babe, it's been 48 hours. I can only handle about another 12 at the most." Husbands don't use this as a weapon to get what you want, the way you want it.

1. It fulfills her womanhood

If a woman considers herself unsuccessful in bed, she will have a difficult time accepting her total womanhood. A wife is more than a mother and homemaker. She is also a sexual partner to her mate. Like a male, if she doesn't succeed in the bedroom she fails in other areas. Why? Few men accept bedroom failure, taking it personally, and they become carnal, nasty, and insulting. Whether or not guys want to admit it, it's true. They want it their way, the way they want it, and they have a tendency to be pushy. They also have mental images of how they want it and if they don't get it, they can slip into sinful behaviors. When you do that you're sending her this message, "I am not satisfied with you. You're not good enough. You need to learn something new because you're not a good sexual partner." The problem is she may be a great sexual partner, but if you have a history of pornographic use, and if you have a history of past sexual experiences, you are wrongly trying to reproduce that in her. Reality and fantasy will never match.

She needs to know she's a good sexual partner. Just like a man, the wife needs a good dose of encouragement about whatever she does in the relationship.

2. It fulfills his sense of manhood

A man usually possesses a stronger ego than a woman. If he's not a man in his own eyes, he's nothing, and somehow his sex drive seems intricately linked to his ego. A man can endure academic, occupational, or social failure as long as he and his wife relate well together in the bedroom, but success in other fields becomes a hollow mockery if he strikes out in bed. To the man, if he's unsuccessful in his bedroom it signals failure in life.

There was a lady who noticed a season when her husband's job wasn't doing well, and he wasn't making as much money as he wanted. Every time he did the bills, she watched him slowly slump. So every two weeks when he'd pay the bills, she'd take him to the bedroom and make love to him. Do you know what that did? It boosted his sense of confidence, his sense of worth, and it made him feel that, even in the midst of his struggles, he was still loved and appreciated. She was one wise woman. She figured out how to minister to him relationally and emotionally.

Don't be deceived by the thin coating of tough masculinity most men wear. Underneath are many emotional needs that only a loving wife can supply. A truly secure woman will convey her sex appeal and satisfaction only to her husband. It gives him great pleasure and, in fact, makes his own sexual pleasure more satisfying when he is assured that he's been mutually enjoyed. (Don't miss that!) It is important that you let him know he's a good lover, you enjoy your sexual times together, and he's pleasing to you. It's important for him to know that because it's tied to his masculinity, his sense of manhood.

Some ladies might say, "He needs to get over it." You can argue that all you want, but it won't happen. God made him that way and you have to learn to work with it. Maturing and meeting each other's needs is what marriage is all about. Telling him to get over it is like telling him to change his biological makeup.

2. It reassures her of her husband's love

The point in which all psychologists agree is that all people have a basic need to be loved. Humans need to be loved and to be intimate. This is generally truer of women than men. Women have a tremendous capacity of love, for both giving and receiving. You need to know there are five kinds of love to minister to their wife; and she needs them all.

a. **Companionship love.** A woman looks upon companionship as a perpetual friendship that keeps going even after the wedding. Just because a couple gets married doesn't mean this is an area no longer cultivated. A man's sex drive shouldn't affect his level of friendship. This type of love is not sexual, but it's vital. She needs to know she's more than a sexual partner. She wants to know you two are best friends.

b. **Compassionate love.** Women are naturally compassionate and this testifies to her need to receive compassion. A wise husband will learn to show empathy when she's emotionally or physically hurting. When you arrive home and see she's had a rough day at work, gently ask her, "How's the day been?" When she says, "It's been really rough," that's the husband's opportunity to make a beneficial choice. "Sounds like it's been hard for you," he says. "I want you to know I care." Then he goes over and hugs her. Men aren't socialized in this culture to do this well, but I'm here to tell you it can be learned.

c. **Romantic love.** Women are much more romantic than men. Men are more romantically tended when they are dating and wanting something. Unfortunately, many times the romance fades after the wedding because they got what they wanted. Women are romantics. Lurking in the heart of every girl, even when she's growing up, is the image of a Prince Charming on a white horse coming to wake up the Princess with her first kiss. But in today's culture with radical feminism at every turn, it's suggested that's not true anymore. That may be true for some individuals, but research shows the majority still want to be mothers with a healthy home. They don't want to build careers. A woman never loses the need to be romanced. She still likes the flowers, the music, the soft lights, dinner out, and a whole host of things. This is where her love tank can be filled, and she can be emotionally nurtured. Keep in mind, romantic love doesn't mean sexual love.

d. **Affectionate love.** Ladies need this—a tender touch, a warm embrace, a hug, or just being held. Again, this is not sexual. One of the biggest gripes women give is, "Oh yeah! He doesn't mind sitting on the couch holding my hand as long as I give in to want he wants." What she needs to know is her husband can have affectionate touching without it leading to intercourse. She'll like the security of knowing she can enjoy your company and your affection without an ulterior motive being involved.

e. **Passionate love.** This deals with her sex drive. I'll explain it in detail in the third reason why lovemaking is significant to the wife.

3. It enhances his love for his wife

Because a man has been endowed by God with an intense sex drive and a conscience—yes, he does have a conscience—the satisfactory relief of that sexual drive without provoking his conscience will enhance his love for the person who makes that possible. Only one person can fulfill both requirements: the wife.

Guys can basically satisfy their sex drive one of four ways. He can do this through intercourse, masturbation, wet dreams, or through homosexuality. Those are primary ways to have an orgasm, but which ones will provoke your conscience? Homosexuality and masturbation irritate your conscience. Wet dreams provoke embarrassment. Intercourse with a woman who's not your wife will also bring guilt. But intercourse with your wife leaves you with no sense of guilt or shame. To enhance your love for your wife, God endowed you with a sex drive that says you do it this way, with this person, in this context, and you will not be ashamed. There will only be a deep sense of love, care, and compassion for that person.

In today's culture, people are going to prostitution, adultery, the internet, masturbating, and all kinds of weird stuff. They get their sex drive release, but they walk away with their conscience provoked. Some might say, "I can do fine without a conscience." I would argue that you can't; you've just seared it so you don't feel it anymore. If it's done the right way, it'll enhance your love for your wife. Anything else can detract from it.

Listen to this: When sex provides only gratification and is followed by guilt, it makes a mockery of what God intended to be a very satisfying experience.

By contrast, the act of intercourse in marriage when performed properly is followed by physical relaxation based on innocence. The reason is because sex is such a necessary part of a man's life and married love preserves the innocence of his conscience. The woman who provides this for her husband will increasingly become the object of his love. Ladies who want the affection and love of their husbands don't purposefully withhold.

Michelle Weiner-Davis, author of *Divorce-busting*, says wives get sick and tired of their husbands not loving them, caring about them, nurturing them, or doing what they want to do. In women's groups she ministers to wives complaining about their husbands, she gives them what sounds like unorthodox advice. "I want you to do something," she tells wives. "For the next two weeks, give him sex two to three times a week. Just do it." These ladies came back afterwards and began reporting, "It's the funniest thing. He started helping around the house, with the kids, and he actually sat and started talking to me this past week." You see, what the wives had been doing was they were withholding, and by withholding he became frustrated, angry, and wasn't bringing love to his wife. Ladies, don't lose sight of this—it's in the act of intercourse your husband's loving you. That's his foundation and the platform for the other acts of love you're looking for.

3. It satisfies her sex drive

Most women need to cultivate passionate love. It's easier for her to express passionate love after the other four needs for love have been satisfied. Do you want her to develop passionate love in a bigger way? Then make sure you minister to her needs for romantic love, affectionate love, companionship love, and compassionate love. Although a woman may not possess as strong or consistent a sex drive as a man, she does have a sex drive. Research indicates that almost all women are more passionate just before, during, or after their monthly menstruation, and, of course, in the middle of the month at the time of highest fertility. Moreover, her sexual pleasure grows throughout the years. As she learns to be uninhibited in her responses to her husband and increasingly learns to experience orgasms, the appreciation and desire for the experience grows. Research shows an interesting difference between men and women. In their early 20s and 30s, men have a high interest in sexual intercourse, which later plateaus in his later 30s. Women's interest in sex doesn't peak until they get into their 30s.

Unlike husbands, wives have sexual seasons in their monthly lives called the menstrual cycle. This is a test for the husband, and he who can pass it will enjoy a vibrant sexual relationship with their wife. Consider the yearly seasons: winter, spring, summer, and fall. In the middle of the menstrual cycle, it's winter, cold and daunting. After winter comes spring when things begin to thaw out and liven up. Things get better because after spring comes summer when things start heating up. It's a time of fun and frivolity. Be prepared though, for after summer comes fall, when things aren't real cold yet but you can see the changing of the season. A guy might be tempted to shut down temporarily and say, "Oh boy, we're in fall right now. I can't wait for spring to show up again." Here's great wisdom: even if you have a winter wife, guys, you need to be a summer husband all the time. Why? Because even if she's at winter, whether it's a menstrual cycle or an attitude, she will thaw out if you maintain a sunny attitude and keep it summer.

4. It reduces friction at home

Another result of a satisfying relationship between a husband and wife is it tends to reduce minor irritations in the home. A sexually satisfied man is usually a contented man. Sometimes a man's irritabilities are a result of his sexual frustrations. I've said this before, but it bears repeating: a wife who withholds is using sex as a weapon. Advice for the guys—if you're not loving, not nurturing, not caring, and are insensitive, it's real difficult for her to desire closeness with you. If you want her to be close, loving, and nurturing in the act of intercourse, you have the responsibility to assure her emotional and relational needs are being ministered to on a consistent basis.

Can she lie there and have you make love to her if you haven't treated her adoringly? Sure. Biologically, she's designed that way. Does she have to be interested? No, her mind could be in Timbuktu while she's just letting you use her body. But who longs for that? Sexual intercourse is designed to be pleasurable, not a chore. Men want their wives to enjoy them just as women want their husbands to find them satisfying. To enjoy sexual satisfaction, husbands you need to minister to your wife's emotional and relational needs of attention, acceptance, affirmation, appreciation, and respect on a consistent basis. When you do this she will reciprocate by wanting to please you. This all goes back to the theory of 'us-ness.' One partner or the other isn't trying to get what they want out of the relationship, but instead, they're striving for what'll be best for both of them. A satisfying sex life reduces friction in the home.

Wives don't use sex as a weapon. A sexually frustrated man has a hard time concentrating, is prone to be edgy, and harder to work with, and, more important, finds it difficult to retain lasting goals. By contrast, the truly satisfied husband refuses to waste his business day on trivia. He wants each moment to count so he can get home to the wife and family who give all his hard work real purpose and meaning.

4. It relaxes her nervous system

Some women who are nervous by nature might find themselves sexually indifferent or negative. Nervousness reduces the desire for sexual intercourse. Our nervous systems are linked to our reproductive organs, and sex provides a much needed relaxant for the nervous system. Healthy sexual function promotes fidelity, fulfillment, and security in the marriage. Why? Well, what is the largest sex organ in the body? Your brain. If your brain is not functioning correctly, neither will your sex organs.

I'm going to address a delicate, but big, problem—that of masturbation. It's destructive because it irritates your conscience. God made intercourse to be with your mate. Orgasm is to be experienced in a relationship, not by a hand or an object. By doing this, you're pairing your brain to the sensation of something other than your mate. Research shows over time that you develop sexual disorders because your brain doesn't respond to the sensation of your mate. Do it God's way so you can spare your conscience and relax the nervous system from tension.

5. It provides life's most exciting experience

Sex is the titanic emotional and physical explosion that culminates the act of marriage. For the husband, it's easily the most exciting experience he ever enjoys on a repeatable basis. Pornography is a cheap, sleazy substitute for intercourse with the one you love and married. Remember to meet her emotional and relational needs so she can enjoy your lovemaking.

5. It provides the ultimate experience for her as well

When properly consummated to orgasm, married love provides a woman with life's most exciting experience. And yes, guys, women enjoy having orgasms. But after talking to hundreds of couples in sex therapy in Texas, I've discovered that orgasms aren't as important to women as they are to men. Now that seems like a foreign concept to a man's mind because you think if she doesn't have one, somehow you didn't do a good job. For guys, his wife's orgasm is tied to his ego; he thinks he's failed. But through therapy experience and research, I've discovered that if she doesn't, it doesn't mean she doesn't want to; her satisfaction is based elsewhere. She is enjoying the closeness, the intimacy, and the time with you.

It's in the act of intercourse and through the orgasmic experiences that the man is showing and giving love. It is at the point where he has his orgasm when he's most vulnerable emotionally. But men, though you are most vulnerable emotionally after the orgasm, she's most vulnerable days or weeks before it happens. You must be ministering to those needs in her relationship, her emotions, and her heart on an ongoing basis because if they're not met, she could perform physically, but it may not be what you were hoping for.

Why did God create sex?

God created sex for two reasons: to propagate the race and to produce mutual ownership.

First, back in the Garden of Eden, God instructed "Be fruitful and multiply." The Lord doesn't consider sex between husband and wife to be a "dirty" thing. He created it for us to enjoy and to bring children into the world. Some people wrongly think that sex is a duty to be performed once married, thus draining the fun out of it.

I once counseled a woman struggling sexually in her marriage. She thought sex was strictly for the sake of having babies. She couldn't fathom the idea it was also designed for pleasure. We asked her to go to her clergyman and get his advice. When he told her it was all right to have intercourse for the fun of it, that shattered her wrong thinking and she relaxed and enjoyed her relationship much more. You see, if we believe something, even if it's wrong, that belief will affect the way we think and feel about it.

According to the Song of Solomon and Proverbs 5:18 and 5:20, sex in marriage is to provide mutual pleasure. Husband and wife don't be afraid to express yourselves sexually to each other.

But it's also to produce mutual ownership, the culmination of what I call 'us-ness.' In 1 Corinthians 7:3-4, the Bible says, "the husband should not deprive his wife of sexual intimacy, which is her right as a married woman, nor should the wife deprive her husband. The wife gives authority over her body to her husband, and the husband also gives authority over his body to his wife." This authority is not for abuse, but to unleash unconditional love on your spouse. It helps develop the uniqueness of a one-flesh relationship. It's ordained by the Creator himself for our enjoyment.

* 18 *

THE ROLE OF A HUSBAND

What does the life of a godly man look like? What is the role of a husband? Unlike what this culture is trying to teach us, there are unique and important responsibilities for the man. The most caustic issue today is the relationship of a man with his wife. Our culture is trying to redefine the timeless roles of a husband, of a man, and of a male's manhood in an effort to make them effeminate. It is also trying to adapt the woman's role so they take on a more masculine role. The husband has different responsibilities from his wife, but he is not better than she is, just as she isn't better than he is. Radical, so-called "women's rights" groups want to portray men as inferior and insignificant. Sadly, some men actually live out those imposed stereotypes, not taking responsibility for finances, for spiritual leadership, or protecting his wife from physical or ideological harm.

We're going to start with a familiar passage of scripture which explains God's design for marriage. In Ephesians 5:21, the Bible says, "And further, you will submit to one another out of reverence for Christ." Unlike what some fringe thinkers believe, wives are not to be their husbands' doormats. One isn't better than the other. To work in unity and with peace and purpose, each spouse submits to the other. A husband's job is to submit to his wife. A wife's job is to submit to her husband.

The next several verses use that foundation to outline the roles of husband and wife. "You wives will submit to your husbands as you do to the Lord. For a husband is head of his wife as Christ is head of his body, the church; He gave His life to be her Savior. As the church submits to Christ, so you wives must submit to your husbands in everything.

"And you husbands must love your wives with the same love Christ showed the church. He gave up His life for her to make her holy and clean, washed by baptism and God's word. He did this to present her to Himself as a glorious church without a spot or wrinkle or any other blemish. Instead, she will be holy and without fault. In the same way, husbands ought to love their wives as they love their own bodies. For a man is actually loving himself when he loves his wife" (Ephesians 5:22-28).

We're going to look at the husband's role first from these verses. Husbands must love their wives with the same love Christ showed the church. The King James Version of the Bible says, "Husbands, love your wives, even as Christ also loved the church, and gave Himself for it" (Ephesians 5:25). Some may take that verse and feel like they must perform spiritual martyrdom. "Well, my job is to die to myself, and even die for her if necessary. That's my job as husband?" It's always—and I really mean always—hard to do anything without any kind of motivation. People won't work well unless they know they'll be compensated with pay. People won't exercise without knowing it'll make them look and feel better. For the husband, what is the motivation for the 'giving himself as Christ gave Himself for the church' idea? Men are purpose-driven. Where women tend to concentrate more on relationships, men strive to accomplish tasks and complete goals. The Lord gives us the reason the husband is to 'give himself,' and to love his wife. It is to fulfill a great purpose in her life. Verse 25 didn't finish the thought; we must go on for the motivation factor. This time we're going to look at the entire context. Men, if you want to accomplish a goal, here's a great one. The Bible says, "And you husbands must love your wives with the same love Christ showed the church. He gave up His life for her to make her holy and clean, washed by baptism and God's word. He did this to present her to Himself as a glorious church without a spot or wrinkle or any other blemish. Instead, she will be holy and without fault." In other words, guys, the reason you die to self—Christ being the model by dying for the church—is because through my right relationship with her and being the example, I can present my wife holy, blameless, washed by the Word. Husbands are to reflect the standard of love Christ established because we'll only be husbands to our wives while we live here on earth; our main job as husbands is to prepare our wives for her spiritual husband, the Lord Jesus Christ.

Before we go on, we're going to look at an overview of two timeless truths concerning sexual roles. Biblical understanding of sexual roles is essential to the survival and success of the Christian family. Mankind was created as sexual beings. Genesis 1:27 says, "He created them male and female." When I talk about sexual roles, I'm specifying gender roles.

Timeless truth #1

Males and females are separate and distinct genders. They are not interchangeable, but unique. Even from a young age, there are biological differences between boys and girls that go beyond their physical bodies. Why am I bringing up this seemingly obvious truth? There are elements in our culture today that say fundamentally there are no differences between men and women. There is actually a movement today that actually says women don't need men. To get explicit, you even hear from lesbian marriages, "We don't need men. All we need is sperm so we can have a baby. We can get that anywhere, but outside of that, we are no different and we don't need men." Whether you like it or not, there are differences between the two genders, and understanding those differences is essential to understanding healthy relationships. Biologically, we're different. The different body distinctions and functions are obvious. Emotionally, we're different. Generally, women are more in touch with their feelings, whereas, for men, we aren't roused by them as consistently. Even relationally we're different. Let's take the example of children. Boys tend to be a little more thinking-oriented and aggressive. Girls will naturally show their nurturing side; that's why you see them walking around with dolls in toy strollers.

God made us different. He made us male and female.

Timeless truth #2

God created the two sexes with distinct purposes in mind. The Bible spells out the husband's role as one created by God and that he is to love and lead his wife and to provide for and protect his family. God created the wife's role for her to nurture her children and support her husband. This truth is also under attack by groups in our culture.

Our culture tells wives that they can have a career just as satisfying and gratifying as their husbands, and if they have children, they don't have to be a stay-at-home mom. Now at the risk of being scathed and isolated, I'm going to say what I believe to be the truth. I'm not saying wives shouldn't work, but it is clear in scripture that when a woman puts her career over her role as mother, she is out of the biblical model. The Bible says a woman is to put her home and children first.

"That's what the Bible says?" you may ask condescendingly. Women were fed the notion that they should compete with men for their jobs, even if that meant to sacrifice the formative years of your young child's life. What many women discovered is that trying to be fulfilled by taking on a man's role did not satisfy. Study shows that a great number of women are leaving the career force to once again be with their children and to support their husbands. I'm not saying don't work. I'm just saying that's not what God designed to be your main priority. The current opinion says you don't have to raise your kids. Let someone else do it. However, results are coming out of kids raised in daycare centers, and it shows their relationships aren't healthy. In your child's young years—around three, four, and five—they are in a bonding stage. Would you rather have them bond with you, or bond with daycare workers who just consider your child part of the job?

Understand also there are no roleless marriages. There are two extremes concerning the perspective of marriage roles. At one extreme, you have the legalistic view which states the husband is head of the home, the wife is the doormat, and the wife and kids must submit and do whatever he says. On the other end of the spectrum, there's the view that says, "Oh no. We're completely equal. I can do what I want, you can do what you want, and we'll have separate checking accounts. You are you, I am me, and we have marriage. If it's a marriage that works for both of us, good, but if it doesn't, we can move on." Even those are roles though, aren't they? There are no roleless marriages. Every marriage has a role, and the health of the marriage depends on the health of the roles you live out.

We're going to look at the different aspects of the biblical role of a husband. What does it really look like?

The role of headship

What does headship mean? Some may think it's being head of the home. Others would say its being an example at home. Could it be setting a standard for forgiveness, resolving conflict, showing nurture and affection, or being sensitive? I don't think any of those are excluded. There may be some guys who wonder what headship looks like, while to others it could be intimidating. Let me tell you a little of my history. The Lord saved me when I was 17 years old when I went to a crusade in a high school gym. During my short journey with Christ afterwards, I sensed God was calling me into the ministry, and I thought that meant being a preacher. I thought of going to a Bible college, but instead I ended up in the United States Navy as a chaplain's assistant. One of my duty stations was in Jacksonville, Florida, and it was there that I visited the First Baptist Church. I received a rude awakening because all the things I was hearing about being a "good Christian" was things I wasn't doing—tithing, praying daily, and Bible study.

A few years later, I got married to a faithful member of that church. My wife had wonderful expectations of me. Guess what they were? She thought I was supposed to pray everyday with her, read the Bible everyday, and lead her in Bible study every day. The fact is I wasn't practicing those things. How could I lead her in these things in this marriage when I didn't implement them in my single life? The pressure of failing my wife drove me to insecurity. I forced myself to do those expected things, and it lasted only six months. I found myself angry at the church, I was angry at her, I hated myself, and I hated God.

After some deep introspection, I finally realized from where all the frustration was coming. I was trying to live up to *her* expectation of what I was supposed to be spiritually.

Finally, I asked her, "Do you believe I love God?"

"Yes," she responded.

"Are you sure?"

"Yes."

"Good. Then He will mature me, not you. It's not your job to grow me. It's His. Now, if you believe I love Him, trust the Lord to mature me, and trust that as He does I'll be doing what I know to do."

Even though I didn't fit her image of what headship should look like, does it mean I wasn't head of the home? Of course not. It just meant I was living out what I knew, and the more I knew over time, the better I could live it out. No one is born with all the wisdom and insight they need for life. We'll be learning until the day we go home to be with the Lord. What I am challenging you to do is enjoy the process. Have you given up on being the leader of your home? Pick yourself up, dust yourself off, and begin to incorporate godly principles and disciple in your life. Are you on the journey to maturity and Christ-likeness? Are you in that process? The Lord is a process-oriented God. He's not an event-oriented God. There is no one event that can make you into all you need to be. He only uses events to create processes. Enjoy the journey of progressing to what He wants you to be.

What does biblical headship mean?

First let me tell you what it doesn't mean. Listen carefully: it doesn't mean ignoring your responsibilities. What predicts distress and divorce is avoidance and withdrawal, and this is typically from the male's part in relationships. When the husband doesn't deal with his issues in the home and ignores responsibility, he's not displaying headship. Headship is taking responsibility for the appropriate choices, decisions, and direction of the marriage and the family. Headship is not an excuse for being passive.

"Well, it'll all work out in the end."

Really? How are you asserting yourself in whatever problem or breakdown is happening?

Sometimes we can get over-spiritual about our headship, after all, the chain of command is God, then husband, and then wife.

"I've been doing what I know to do, and now I'll just trust God to do what needs to be done."

That sounds good, but the Lord won't perform your responsibility for you. He'll equip you to live out your role as a responsible husband.

"I'm praying about what needs to be done in this marriage," you might say.

"That's great! But while you're praying about it, what else are you doing?"

Praying with no desire for change accomplishes nothing. Twenty years from now I could ask, "You still praying about it?"

"Oh yeah. I'm still praying about it."

Do you know why nothing's changed? You haven't initiated anything.

I could imagine the Lord saying, "You continue praying, but in the meantime I know three or four different things you could be doing to enhance your marriage relationship. Why don't you choose one?"

"Well, I'm waiting for you to tell me."

"No," the Lord replies, "I've given you a brain. Use it. You know My Word, and whatever decision you need to make, make it. But don't sit around passively and blame Me for not being responsible with the blessing of marriage."

In a previous chapter we learned how complex and powerful the brain is. The Lord provided you a brain for complicated problem solving. He wants you to use it. Now, that doesn't mean we're to write off prayer, or to not seek direction from the Lord or from a godly counselor. But with all the tools the Lord's given us—our brain, His Word, prayer, counseling—there's no reason we should shrink back and not take hold of the honor and responsibility of headship. I am responsible, whether I like it or not, to deal with issues.

Sometimes you may come up against opposition. Headship involves dealing responsibly with communication concerning issues also.

A while back, I really wanted a dog, so I visited the Humane Society and saw several dogs I'd love to have.

When my wife and I saw each other at home I told her, "I went to the Humane Society and saw several dogs we could choose from."

"We're not getting a dog," she replied sharply.

I could feel anger rising up. "You don't make that decision," I said.

"Oh yes I do. This is my house, too, and we're not getting a dog."

I took a deep breath I could feel the emotional part of my brain wanting to take over and say some ugly stuff. I had to shift to the thinking brain by sticking to the communication skills. "So what you're saying is you don't want a dog."

After going through the communication skills, I ended by saying, "You know, honey? This family is bigger than just you, and I respect the fact that you don't want a dog, and I heard you don't want a dog because of these reasons. However, it seems to me you don't tell me what I can or cannot do, because I don't tell you what you can or cannot do. It's not biblical. That isn't the way things work. God doesn't tell you what you can or can't do. He lays out a standard that says either you obey Me or you don't. We determine our consequences. I don't appreciate the fact you are telling me what I can or can't do. We need to sit down and talk about this because the kids and I want a dog, but I am also willing to give on some issues."

If I just sat back and done nothing with that conflict I would have been harboring resentment and bitterness which would have come out in other ways which wouldn't have been mature. I had to deal with it right then and there.

The next morning she came to me and asked, "Will you forgive me?"

"For what?"

"For telling you what you can or can't do with the dog issue. I was wrong."

"Sure," I said, "You're forgiven."

We didn't get that dog. It wasn't the right time, and timing is everything. Will we get one? I believe so. But whatever her stance, I will always be respectful. Headship means leading respectfully.

Headship means you possess the authority to lead your home. Our ability to lead and exert authority is only as it relates to Christ's model of leadership. When you want to look to what a leader does, you look at what Christ did. Christ doesn't beat you down verbally. Should you do that to your wife? I was talking to a guy who dealt with this problem. His wife took a vacuum cleaner bag and dumped it in some dirt outside their house. For something inconsequential as that, he went into a rage, started throwing things, and called her a whore.

"I have the right to do that," he said.

"Why?" I asked.

"Because I am the head of the home. She shouldn't do that."

"No! You don't have the right to do what you're doing. You are grossly out of line, and if you've been doing this for years, no wonder your marriage stinks."

The standard of leadership is Christ Jesus. Since I'm supposed to lead and exert authority, ask yourself if Christ went around calling people names and putting them down. Since He wouldn't do those things to you, what gives you the right to do those things to somebody else?

Using authority to serve

The Lord's ways are opposite of mankind's ways. Mankind says authority means everybody should be doing something for me. The Lord says authority means doing things for others. Biblical headship assumes responsibility for others. Our leadership is to the good of the family, not ourselves.

What are some ways to live out your servant leadership?

To glorify your wife

To reiterate, Ephesians 5:26-28 says, "He gave up His life for her to make her holy and clean...He did this to present her to Himself a glorious church without a spot or wrinkle or any other blemish. Instead, she will be holy and without fault. In the same way, husbands ought to love their wives as they love their own bodies. A man actually loves himself when he loves his wife." When Christ died and rose again for the church, He didn't do it for Himself. He did it for the good of those who trust Him for salvation. The Bible pictures Christ as the groom and us as the church, or the bride. But there was major conflict in this relationship. Sin put contention between the bride and the Father. The Father created us and loved us, but because of sin, we were alienated from Him. So what did the Groom do? He stepped in to solve the conflict between the Father and the bride. Even though Jesus was blameless in this issue, He became the initiator to solve the problem.

Whenever there's a conflict in your home, why don't you do the same? Why don't you be the initiator to resolve the conflict instead of the one who keeps it going?

Christ died and rose again to glorify the church. Husbands must die to their selfishness and agendas, and rise again under Christ's leadership to bring their families to success. Christ communicated forgiveness. As a servant leader, husbands must learn how to also communicate forgiveness. One example of spiritual leadership and initiating forgiveness is to confirm your wife's beauty. Don't make your wife question her beauty.

"I think you could lose a few more pounds."

"Wow. Doesn't that lady over there look attractive?"

Remember the Bible says the power of life and death is in your words. You can tear a person's image down by what you say and how you say it.

What you say about your wife or to your wife reflects a lot about you. If you decided to marry her and made your vows for better or worse, and you have a tendency to put her down, you're telling everybody you're a poor decision maker and a poor steward of what you've got. Confirm her beauty.

Prioritize your marriage relationship over other relationships

There is so much to be said on this but let me summarize it this way: my job, my friends, my golf, my paintball, or any other hobbies, people, or activities aren't to be priorities over my marriage. My children aren't to take priority over my marriage. Your church doesn't even take priority over your marriage. This doesn't mean you don't worship or serve the Lord; it means don't use religion as an excuse to abandon your marriage. It would be hypocritical to be actively involved in your church when your marriage relationship is suffering and things aren't right at home. God doesn't call you to be perfect. He calls you to be faithful. Prioritize the marriage relationship over others.

Provide care to your wife

This goes beyond three square meals, a roof over her head, and clothing. She needs more than the physical things of life. She has intimacy needs. She needs attention. She needs respect. She needs affection. When you minister to those needs, you minister care. To provide for her financially while having her die emotionally means you're failing as a husband and a leader. When we care for her we build her self-esteem. When you meet her intimacy needs you show her she's got value. When you invest time, attention, and affection in her you give her a sense of worth. When you don't care for those needs, emotionally she withers. The consequences of your care for her will be your responsibility. The pattern for you caring for her means she'll reciprocate. If you treat her like trash, don't expect much love in return.

What does God intend for you?

The Lord intends a man to be part of a greater union. Marriage is bigger than you and your wife; the ultimate goal is a sense of Us-ness. Being a real man is being focused on Us-ness in your marriage. Us can do so much more than either my wife or my self could do separately. Real men understand the importance of their wives' roles in their own personal development. Your wife should be your closest friend and your most trusted confidant. Are you nurturing your relationship in such a way? A wife helps a husband mature emotionally and spiritually. Your wife helps you find deeper and different dimensions of God that you wouldn't know on your own. A marriage is designed to be a team, with the husband as the leader, but with the wife adding attributes that weren't present when you were single. You can accomplish goals and overcome obstacles more easily and joyfully when you as a husband take the responsibility to create Us-ness in the marriage. The wife is naturally inclined to do that, but since you're the leader, it's your responsibility.

If we're going to be godly men, role models, and spiritual leaders, we're going to give up ourselves as Christ gave Himself for the church. He gave and reaped the rewards of His sacrifice. When we, as husbands and leaders of the home, sacrifice, it is for the success and well-being of the relationship. There are three things that need to be prominent in our lives as leaders.

Self-denial

Jesus Christ, the King of the Universe, laid aside the privilege of deity and stepped into time. He became a man, endured the same hardships as any other, and even denied Himself to the point of dying for us—suffering the wrath of God so we wouldn't have to. Servant leaders deny themselves for the good of the family.

For theoretical and metaphorical purposes, let's reason this out. If you were to deny yourself, what would it look like in your marriage? If you were practicing self-denial in your marriage, what would it look like? What would you be doing differently?

Would communication improve? Of course. You'll put the relationship first instead of wanting your own way or feeling like you've got to compete and win against your spouse. When issues or conflict arise, you'll turn to the communication skills, asking things like "So what you are saying is..." When you're denying yourself, you want to solve the problem, not inflame it, and create an atmosphere of peace and safety. Self-denial uses the thinking part of your brain, not the emotional component. Don't let your anger, resentment, bitterness, or disappointment control you, but instead look for the healthy solution to any problem plaguing your marriage.

Would your practical application improve? You better believe it. With right thinking comes right attitude and right actions. Your wife desires more quality time with you. What might you do? You might not go play golf one day. You could avoid going to work when you don't have to, and stay home with her. You might even decide to go to the restaurant she likes instead of the one you like.

Think back to your dating time. When you were dating her and trying to win her over, you did a lot of things you might not have preferred because of your feelings for her. Then a few years into marriage, you quit doing those things. You stop trying to win the prize when you've got her. You made her feel important then, why don't you now? Practice self-denial and continually try to win her over. Selfishness accomplishes nothing but separation in your relationship. Self-denial is the model Christ set for us to follow. When you live a life of self-denial, there'll be nothing to regret.

Sacrificial action

Christ gave his life for those whom He loved, and He loves us in times when we are absolutely unlovable. Husbands are called upon daily to give up their desires and die to self. That is tough to do, especially when you feel like yelling. Especially when you feel like walking away. Especially when you feel like giving up. Remember, it's not about you or your spouse; it's about your Us-ness. God created everybody differently. Our problem is we see the differences as hindrances instead of marriage enhancements. Our differences add to the Us-ness of the relationship. Sacrificial action is important because it doesn't focus on what the individual wants or needs, it focuses on what the couple needs as a whole. When sacrificial action is part of who I am, I'll do bizarre things like dying to myself. I might esteem my wife more highly than myself. Why? When I'm practicing this in my relationship, I'm doing something that's the best for us. When she feels loved by me, she'll feel love toward me.

When you practice self-denial, it leads to sacrificial action. When you instill sacrificial actions into your life and attitudes, you're growing and nurturing the love and trust in the relationship. When you show your wife that you actually do care for her, not with words only, but by actions, she'll be willing to show you the attention you desire.

A servant's heart

Jesus continually set aside his own desires to serve others. In the same way, husbands should surrender their own agendas and their hobbies to serve their wives and meet their needs. "What about my needs and my desires?" you may be asking. Let me tell you a story.

A long while ago, I used to do model building, paintball and other hobbies, but I did them so often I put those before my marriage. When placing these hobbies before my relationship, an atmosphere of aloneness was created which created distance and disconnectedness in our marriage. My wife and I had a long talk about it one day, and I talked to the Lord, saying, "I have to make a conscious effort not to do these things and put the marriage first, even if that means I can't do these other things I want to do." So that's what I did.

What I found out later was that when she felt security and confidence in the marriage, and she experienced attention, acceptance, and affection, she would say to me, "Why don't you go play some paintball?"

Things changed and there was more freedom in the relationship because she felt if she needed me, that I would be there. I invested in her, and later received the dividends of it.

What happens if I fail?

I am not called to be perfect. I'm called to be faithful. There are certain things that motivate me in my relationship life. I want Christ to be proud of me, and I want my wife to be proud of me. Relationships are complicated and complex. Situations within them can be tiring and sometimes intimidating, but when we obey the Lord and live out the life He's designed for us you can sense Him saying, "Good job, son! I know this is tough for you, but you're doing great. I'm with you and I'm cheering you on."

With excitement, your spirit can say, "Okay, Father. Then it's you and me, and as long as You're proud of me, that's all that matters."

As husbands, we won't always do things perfectly though. Your life is like a bicycle race. If you're faithful you're always gaining ground. There may be times when you wreck along the way. What do you do then? When you fall, you don't say, "I can't believe I fell. I've got to start over." The Lord has no interest in you starting over. He wants you to pick yourself up, learn from your mistake, and keep pressing forward.

We all mess up one way or the other. You could wreck several times along this race called life, but that doesn't make you a failure. The Christian walk is a progression, so just keep moving forward and you'll make it to the finish line.

When you fall, the Lord asks, "What did you do wrong? What are you going to do different next time? Obey my Word and keep moving."

Your wife knows if you are sincere, and she knows how to forgive you if you make mistakes. Falling down in the race shouldn't be the pattern of our lives. It should be the exception. When you love your wife, and she knows it because of your actions and attitudes toward her, she won't hold an occasional mistake against you.

You ultimately decide if you are a failure. How's that? The only time you truly fail is when you quit trying to be all that the Lord designed you to be.

How to be a good husband

What determines if you're a good husband is how well you follow the example of Christ. As human beings, we can suffer from unjust criticism, misunderstanding, or acting out of ignorance. Christ is our example, and He's given us directions in His Word concerning how to prevail as a success to our spouse. The following are guaranteed ways of how to be a good husband.

Honor your wife

Everyone wants to feel important. The spouse relationship is not different. Husband, you love your wife. She must be exalted and never dethroned. The measure of your love for your wife should equate to Christ's love for the church. It's a sacrificial love. What's so important is that you don't just love your wife, but you show her that love. When you were a child, would you like to know your parents loved you or would you rather feel they loved you? Is there any difference in marriage? Would you rather know your spouse loves you or would you rather feel love? Feeling the love is evidence that love exists at the moment. So show your love. All life manifests itself. As certainly as a live tree will put forth leaves in the spring, so certainly will living love show itself. Just because you love someone doesn't mean you're showing that love, and it doesn't mean they're feeling it. Love is no good to your mate unless they can feel it.

Suffer for your wife if need be

Suffering for your wife isn't contemporary thinking among men today, but remember salvation is not immunity from humanity. In humanity there'll be rough times, trying times, and times we must endure. Sometimes it takes working long hours to supply for the bills temporarily. Other times, you may need to help your wife bear an emotional load she's been carrying by patiently being beside her and not trying to solve the problem. If she needs a problem solved, she'll ask. So many times she wants to know you care enough to sacrifice time for things that really aren't important to you.

Study to keep her young

It's not work, but worry, that wears. Keep yourself between her and all harm. If you walk carefully in the way of righteousness, you can shield her from canker and care. Study to keep her young. Become a student of your wife. When I started to do this, I began to understand her in a better way, and I began to understand what it was that she liked. I learned my wife liked photography. She'd always liked it, but couldn't do it because she didn't have the equipment. When I discovered it, I went out and bought her a camera, and she blossomed doing what she loved. My goal is to help her become all she wants to be.

Help her to bear burdens

Galatians 6:2 says, "Bear ye one another's burdens, and so fulfill the law of Christ." Your wife doesn't need to carry the burdens on her own. We are to bear one another's burdens. My wife needs my help. Just because I'm the head of the home and the breadwinner doesn't mean she doesn't need help with parenting, with chores, or with responsibilities. She needs my support. There are times I don't need to fix things for her, because some things she can fix on her own, but she needed to know that when she was struggling in the area of parenting, or anywhere else for that matter, that I was along side her bearing that burden with her. The first crisis of mankind was aloneness. Can you imagine bearing a burden alone? If I bear the burden with her, she's not bearing that burden alone.

Make yourself helpful by thoughtfulness

Remember to bring into the house your smile and sunshine. It's good for you and it cheers up the house. You can either be a thermostat or a thermometer. What does a thermometer do? It reads temperature. What does a thermostat do? It sets the temperature. If you have a winter-wife, you can either read her and react, or you can be a thermostat. You can be a summer-husband and eventually she'll thaw out. Just because she's a winter-wife doesn't mean you have to be a winter-husband. You can change your attitude and still function as a thoughtful, helpful, and cheery person. You can change things.

Study your own character as a husband

Are you seeking to multiply the joys of your wife as well as supporting her? Make yourself a role-model husband that will help your wife to be a model wife. The first person you need to look at when there's a problem is yourself. If you're not sure what to think when you consider yourself, be bold enough to ask for feedback in what others, particularly your wife, see in you. I have some core people that I implicitly trust that I will periodically ask, "What do you see me doing wrong? How can I better this area of my walk?" Or I may share with them a conflict going on in my marriage. I must be willing to listen. I realized I used to be quick to blame my wife for any problem in our marriage when I should have looked at my own life, change what I'm doing or how I'm acting, and thus bring change to the problem. The real question is: am I willing to be humble, suffer a little bit, put my pride aside, and ask myself if maybe I'm a part or the cause of the problem?

Seek to refine your nature

It's not exaggeration to say many men have wives much more refined than themselves. If you're honest, your wife will make you a much better man. She will make you a much better husband. She will dress you much better than you ever thought that you'd ever dress.

Preserve the gentleness and refinement of your wife as a rich legacy for your children by lifting yourself to higher levels and standards. Be a gentleman as well as a husband. The soul of gentlemanliness is a kindly feeling toward others which prompts them to desire your presence.

* 19 *

THE ROLE OF A WIFE

When you think of the role for women—the role of the wife—what kind of things come to your mind, what kind of statements, or pictures? She's an encourager, a nurturer, and the heart of the home. It's important for men to understand a wife is your barometer for the health of the relationship. When your wife starts saying things like, "We really need to talk. Things don't seem right," you want to heed that because women are nurturers of relationships. Since they are the nurturers of the relationship, they are more discerning of the relationship's health. You'll want to listen to her words, and not take them personal. What she may be saying is, "I want to feel more connected, and there is something that is keeping us from being more connected."

The wife is often the encourager or the cheerleader for her husband when he's discouraged. She is supportive of him in his endeavors. Wives can be patient, enduring souls which win over their husbands with a humble spirit, quite unlike the crass, loud misrepresentations of wives you see on sitcoms.

In 1 Peter 3:1-2, the Bible says, "In the same way, you wives must accept the authority of your husbands, even those who refuse to accept the Good News. Your godly lives will speak to them better than any words. They will be won over by watching your pure, godly behavior."

Instead of nagging, yelling, screaming, and complaining, the wife will change him through quietness of spirit rather than being verbal and confrontational. That's interesting because the tendency is to do the opposite. If she wants to change her husband, be quiet. I've noticed with my wife, that she pulled back and became quiet when she disagreed with something I was doing. She took the problem to the Lord, and ended up getting the positive results because the Lord dealt with me instead of her. That habit actually made things better for us when she started doing that.

We're going to look at three important scriptures concerning the wife then we're going to talk about the aspects in detail.

The creation of women

...but for Adam there was not found a helper suitable for him. So the Lord God caused a deep sleep to fall upon the man, and he slept. Then He took one of his ribs and closed the flesh at that place, and the Lord fashioned into a woman the rib which he had taken from the man and brought her to the man (Genesis 2:20-22).

The infamous verse

Wives, submit to your husbands, as to the Lord. For the husband is the head of the wife, as Christ is the head of the church: the body of which He is the Savior. Now as the church submits to Christ, so also wives should submit to their husbands in everything (Ephesians 5:22-24). This is the infamous verse that everyone quotes and says your job is to be submissive. But realize she isn't submitting solely to her husband, but to the authority of Jesus Christ.

An unpopular philosophy

Encourage young women to love their husbands, to love their children, to be sensible, pure, workers at home, kind, being subject to their husbands, that the Word of God may not be dishonored (Titus 2:4-5). This is an unpopular philosophy today. There is nothing wrong with women in the workplace, but why do you think the scripture lists these attributes for the woman's role? Verse 5 emphasizes why—that the Word of God may not be dishonored. People may not like this teaching, especially in today's contemporary culture, but I'm not going to make apologies for what the Lord says. So with that said, there are three principles we're going to look at.

A wife is called to be a helper to her husband

Every woman must understand how much her husband needs her. Society considers "Helper" a demeaning word. What does the Lord mean when He refers to being a helper? It means to encourage, support, and be strong where he is weak. Just as wives are to be helpers to their husbands, so husbands are to be helpers to their wives. God ordained the woman's role to come along side and be a helper to your husband in whatever gifts or calling God has given him, thus encouraging and supporting him. It doesn't mean you're at home barefoot, pregnant, and staying with the kids; it does require you don't put your career over your role as a wife and mother.

Let's talk about being a mother for just a moment. There is an abundance of research that is out after a 20 year study of kids who stayed in daycare. The study shows that daycares are not healthy relationally for the family. These kids aren't bonded to their parents; they're bonded to the workers. Because of this there are many psychological and emotional disturbances that occur. I'm not saying don't put your kids in daycare. What I am saying is we have fooled and deluded ourselves into believing all this is good for our upward mobility, when all it does is undermine the integrity and original intent of what the family was supposed to be.

Wives are called to be submissive

Before we begin, let's look at this word—submissive. The Greek word of submission is **hupatosa**, which means to place or arrange under. Submission is not blind obedience. Ladies don't have to blindly obey what a husband says.

In my practice, there was a lady who married this guy who was controlling about the way she looked and about the finances. Unaware of his shady dealings, she was clueless that they were $70,000 in debt and that he was borrowing money from some mysterious characters. She started receiving phone calls from guys trying to collect on debts. When she understood some of the underhanded things going on, she kept them secret, trying to be loyal to her husband. One day, she wrote a check to get some supplies for the children (they had three kids), and the bank said the account had been closed out. She wasn't sure what her husband's problems were, but now those dark dealings were messing with the kids' welfare. She couldn't cover for him anymore, so she came to my office.

"I need to tell you some secrets," she started, and shared with me the difficulties in their relationship and weird things her husband was dealing with outside the home.

"Here is what you're going to do," I instructed. "You are going to tell your parents everything that is taking place. You will then call his parents and tell them everything that is taking place. Once you've made those calls, you will tell him you are leaving. You're not ending the marriage, but you will be leaving the marriage for a while until he decides what is going to be more important—his marriage or his secret associates. You will not stay there and suffer and allow the kids to suffer without food or clothing because of his wrong choices."

You need a support system. It's hard to just get up and leave. Make sure trustworthy people who care will be there to help. Both sets of parents confronted him, and she returned on that day. She told him, "You have one week to decide what you're going to do, or I leave."

Fortunately, he called me. "I need help," he said.

He was about to lose everything. If he's not willing to protect the marriage and the family, somebody's got to. When husband defaults, it falls to the ladies because you can't let the children suffer. Submission is not blind obedience.

Neither is submission silent suffering. You don't have to put up with his foolishness or his issues that are negatively impacting you or the children. You have the right to stand against unrighteousness and wrong behavior.

Submission isn't something you have to do. It should be something you want to do. Submission is a voluntary subordination to a recognized authority. That doesn't mean he's better than you, that he's over you, or that you are unequal to him. The Bible makes it clear that husbands and wives are equal in the inheritance which is to come. We are equal.

The Lord designed life so in the scheme of it there are always authorities. I have a boss here at work—my pastor. If I do some things that are against the rules he's established, I'll receive consequences. If I keep doing those things, he'll fire me. That's just the way life is if you go against your boss at work. Does that mean your boss is better than you? No. It just means you recognize that even though he isn't better or worse than you, he is the boss and has a positional authority. It is the same in marriage. There is a positional authority. The husband has to be accountable and responsible before God for what happens at home. The Lord looks to the man to assure the health of the family relationships. So the husband is not better than the wife, but he is the divinely appointed authority of the home.

Although a wife is responsible to God for her submission, her husband is to lead in such a way that it makes it reasonable and enjoyable for her to follow. If wives are to submit, what kind of husband do they want to submit to? How hard would it be to submit to a husband who loves you, builds you up, and encourages you? How about a man who is leading you in the godly things of life? It is much easier to live out the role of a wife when the husband is responsible for his role.

Let me add an interesting footnote. Decades ago, it became popular for women to rebel against the thought of submitting to their husbands. The most radical of feminists, Patricia Ireland, the leader of the "Now Gang" who was outspoken against marriage and men, got married. For decades, she emphasized hating men, beating up men, and putting down the role of men. In her sixties, she got married and just undid all she had taught for 32 years. Her issues and her views have caused a lot of damage in our culture, and people have bought into that way of thinking. How interesting is it that the most outspoken person about marriage and the women's role, has now become a part of what she stood against.

Wives are called to make mothering a priority

My wife doesn't work now, but she worked for a number of years until we had children. Although I thought she could still work, she was convinced she shouldn't.

"You can be a good mother and still provide an income," I said.

We argued about it until the first baby was born. I went to her and admitted the Lord had urged me to have her stay at home. She'd never argued much before although she made her views clear. She quietly took the subject to the Lord in prayer, and He changed me. I was scared. How was I going to provide for my family on one income? I discovered the Lord is more than sufficient to supply. As a couple, we decided that our family was more important than an extra income. If I don't have the latest model of TV or the newest DVD's, that's fine. I don't want to be like my dad when he died. On his deathbed, he had his Rolls Royce, his helicopter, his airplane, but he also had broken relationships with all his children. I don't want to die that way. If I don't have the things, but I have the relationships when I die, I'll die at peace with my family, my wife, and my God.

Your children and your home need your time, attention, and painstaking devotion. If you allow your career to get in the way of your mothering, I think you're out of God's will. I'm not saying you shouldn't have a career. I'm saying that shouldn't be your main priority.

You can raise your children or you can let those people down there at Little Johnny Jumper Junior's Daycare Center do it for you. If they do raise your children, they will bond with your child, they will experience your child's first words, and your child will consider them less of a stranger than you. The primary psychological developmental need of a child is to bond early (in the first six years) to their parents, particularly the mother.

President Roosevelt was quoted, "The most honorable and desirable task which can beset any woman is to be a good and wise mother in a home marked by self-respect and forbearance. Her very name stands for loving unselfishness and self-abnegation and, in any society fit to exist, is thought of with associations which remember it holy."

The whole issue of mothering is a powerful one that has gone by the wayside in our culture.

As a side note, fathering is just as important of an issue. Let's not make the mistake that all the responsibility for the children's well-being is on the shoulders of mom. There are 20 million fatherless kids in this culture. The gangs in America are nothing more than a symbolic role of an absent father in that boy's life. Seventy-two percent of men in prison today came from fatherless homes. Fathering is such a powerful issue that it affects the animal kingdom also, not just the human race. Many years ago, *60 Minutes* did a special on a certain group of elephants in Kenya. A couple decades ago, there was an explosion of elephant births on a particular African range. When the pachyderms began to get more mature, wildlife crews decided to relocate the younger elephants to different ranges so they could start herds of their own. For 10 years after the relocation, the crews began to find a rash of mysterious hippo and rhinoceros death in certain wildlife preserves. After thorough investigation, they discovered it was these adolescent elephants which had been killing the other animals.

An elephant expert came in and said, "I can tell you why they're doing that. Ten years ago, when you relocated the elephants, do you understand what you did? The bull elephant, though not in the herd, is always on the outside of the herd watching the younger ones. If a young elephant gets out of line, the bull straightens it up. What happened was when they were removed from the influence of the male bull elephants their natural tendency of the younger ones is to be aggressive. When you put them back around bull elephants over time their behavior will be reshaped."

If even in the animal kingdom the influence of the adult male shapes the behavior of the young, how are we so clueless to not realize that the absence of fathers in the home being involved, nurturing, and raising boys to have masculine roles is creating a violent group of youth? The role of both parents, both father and mother, are vital to raising a well-rounded, healthy child.

How to be a good wife

You may have heard the phrase "Behind every great man is a great woman." Women can accomplish great things on their own, but they also empower and encourage their husbands to achieve phenomenal results. If one of the most esteemed and honored positions of a woman is being a wife, there are actions to help them be their best.

Reverence your husband

The husband sustains, by God's order, a position of dignity, as head of the family. He may not be worthy sometimes, and He may not act like a husband sometimes, but reverence him as a husband anyway. That is just his role. Even if he is unlovable, love him.

Does that mean you have to have sex with him? No.

Are you to use sex as a weapon? No, don't do that either. That is destructive to any marriage.

A wife loves as naturally as the sun shines. Love is your best weapon. You conquered him with that in the first place, and you might be able to win him back with it, too. Nagging and contention will not win him over. The principle I tell women is the same thing I share at men's conferences.

I tell them, "If you want to keep your wife's love throughout the years, then you keep it by doing the very same things that you won it with." Don't conceal your love for him. If he's crowded with care and too busy to notice your love, you need to give all the greater attention to securing his knowledge of your love. Don't withhold it. Always show it. Even if he seems preoccupied, display you care, and don't take it personal if he doesn't respond the way you hoped he would. When the timing's right he'll reciprocate. Though it may seem he doesn't notice, your love is being registered.

Cultivate personal attractiveness

This has nothing to do with your outward looks; this means storing in your mind knowledge of passing events with a good idea of the world's general advance. If you read nothing and make no effort to make yourself attractive through conversation or problem solving, you'll soon sink down to a dull lack of stupidity. The reality is some wives may say, "All I do is stay home and raise the kids." Real attractiveness is when you invest some time in yourself to become emotionally and spiritually mature. Conversations have many levels; the highest level of communication is the discussion of ideas. Be read up, be knowledgeable. There are too many stereotypes about ditsy women who don't use their brains. Believe it or not, husbands like intelligent conversation, especially in the non-threatening atmosphere of the home. Men love physical intimacy because of the physical makeup of a man, but real attraction comes from intellectual intimacy. Keep your minds stimulated and growing, and keep the conversations interesting and informative.

Maintain yourself physically

A man is sight-oriented. Where women aren't stimulated solely by physical appearance, this is major for guys. When you were encouraging his attention while courting or dating, you didn't neglect the tidiness of your clothing or the preparation of your hair. You never greeted him with a ragged dress or soiled hands. Why not try to look just as captivating to him now? It catches his attention, and it shows him that you respect yourself as an individual. Keep yourself at your best; that's how you won him.

Don't forget the power of incidental attentions

A little time spent by your husband's side without actually being busy with either work or plans or complaints is not wasted.

Sometimes, if he is doing something and you show attention in even the smallest way, it makes a world of difference. It's true that "it's the little things that matter." When I would be reading one of my Civil War books or playing a computer game, my wife Luella would stay away, making me think she was uninterested in me or my world. Every once in a while, she'll come over, sit down, and watch. She'll just sit there while I do what I'm doing. This is incidental attention and that means a lot. What ends up happening is I stop what I'm doing, and we spend time talking and visiting. It's wonderful. Don't think just because he's busy you can't be there. If he's watching the news, go sit with him, and just be there with him.

I have an article in my office called, *He Might Be Teething*. Have you ever been around a baby that's teething? It cries a lot and doesn't exhibit the best of attitudes. Since you know he's teething, what's your attitude toward the baby? Do you beat him because he is yelling and screaming? You don't say, "Stop it!" You know he's teething so you tend to be a little more patient, sensitive, and comforting. Sometimes your husband is teething. Don't personalize this. It could be due to bad results at work, getting in a fight with his parents, or just feeling under the weather. Be a little more compassionate and sensitive, most likely it's because of outward circumstances that he may be touchy, not because he's dissatisfied with you.

Study your husband's character. He does have his peculiarities, but that's just part of being a human being. He may even have unhealthy traits. Remember, it's not your job to change him. Ask the Lord, He'll do a complete work on your husband. When you study him, and until the Lord removes some unhealthy habits from him, you will recognize what they are and react appropriately. You can avoid hours of friction this way.

This is the culmination of what it means to live out the role of a wife. A woman chooses to submit to her husband, because when she looks past her husband, she sees the Lord Jesus saying, "Ultimately, you aren't doing this for him, but for Me." The reason you choose to put yourself under your husband's headship is because when you look at him, you see the Lord standing behind him. Your attitude would speak, "Father, I am doing this for You because I want to please You."

Groups and ideologies are trying to redefine the role of the wife in society today. It says it's completely different than what the Lord created it to be. I would argue that as much as you want what God wants, then you must live what He asks us to live. If we do this, even though it is against the current culture, blessings will come in a far greater way than you would ever imagine.

* 20 *

LIFE PRIORITIES

We've heard John Lennon sing, "All you need is love." We've seen a bumper sticker using religious symbols as letters saying, "Co-exist." People talk about world peace. Popping up everywhere are human rights organizations and civil liberty unions. All of these ideas and all these organizations urge mankind to live in harmony, to respect your fellow man, and let people have their rights. With so much time and energy spent on working toward peaceful relationships between all people and nationalities, why does it seem peace is less present than ever before?

We turn on the news in time to hear that there's been another rape, another murder, another theft, and another atrocious act toward a member of the human race. People shrug off their responsibilities and, for convenience sake, destroy the lives of defenseless unborn children. A dictator doesn't like a certain people group and tries to wipe them out through a cruel act of genocide. Individuals lie to each other, slander each other, and belittle folks of whom they're jealous. Why does it seem the human race, despite all the urging to accept each other, is plunging deeper into an environment of violence and hatred?

In one simple explanation, it's because there is no connectedness in relationships.

"Oh, what are you talking about?" you may ask.

Where there's no love, no respect, and no association, people become faceless objects in your path. When was the last time you spent some time with your neighbor next door or across the street, got to know his family, and learned about the struggles and dreams in his life? If something tragic were to happen to him and his family, would he be missed or just a subject of conversation around the water cooler? If someone who lives that close can be a stranger, what would make people of different ideologies pay respect to those they don't know? If people haven't had responsible relationships at home why would they respect an individual's home or person if that person has something they want to take?

Of course, it almost goes without saying that the reason people do sinful things is because they have sinful hearts. In the last 40 years, this country has taken a steep slide away from the principles of God and the results can be seen everywhere. When people neglect the ways of the Lord, they no longer have His detailed Word that directs them into right relationships with God and with others. Thus we have a generation who is disconnected, self-centered, and insecure. With those obstacles it's not surprising relationships are shallow and disposable today.

People are trying to meet the longings of their heart, but can't figure out how. For some, they try it through working incessantly, hoping this will satisfy them. Others turn to alcohol or to drugs, thinking if they can't get their needs met then at least they don't have to be cognizant or responsible for their frustration. Still some turn to people, not for relationship, but to quell a loneliness or a lust they want to satisfy. Everyone has core emotional needs: comfort, acceptance, affection, appreciation, approval, attention, affirmation, respect, encouragement, security, and support. These needs are programmed into us at conception. Like food, air, water, and shelter, these needs are biologically based. The difference is that you cannot meet these needs on your own. They are met only in relationships.

As we see people who walk by with blank expressions, hear people curse at their spouse and kids for the smallest infraction, and people who ask, "Hey, how are you?" and keep walking without waiting for any response, what could be the great disconnect? Why have people turned so inward that they know how to get closer to fictional characters on television than the real live people in their lives? And why do some people do the wackiest, most unhealthy things for themselves and their relationships today.

The answer: pain. And they have no knowledge of how to escape it.

The pain comes from not having needs met.

There are four basic human needs that must be met for people to live healthy and enjoy life: spiritual needs, intellectual needs, emotional needs, and physical needs. When any of these needs arise, they are met through relationships with God and with others. It isn't healthy or wise for a person to lock themselves alone in their house, hidden from the woes of the world, and think they can think and live vibrantly.

Interestingly, each need demands the correct commodity in order to satisfy it. What do I mean? An emotional need demands an emotional commodity. A physical need demands a physical commodity.

Let's say I walked downtown one evening and a homeless man came up to me and said, "I haven't eaten anything in a week. Can you help me?"

What kind of need does he have? A physical need.

"The Lord your God will supply your every need," I replied. "God bless you."

What I said wasn't wrong, but it was the wrong commodity for his need. His physical need of hunger demanded that he have something to eat. I offered him a spiritual commodity for a physical need. In truth, the Lord would have given me the privilege to provide for that wanting man, but because I wasn't sensitive to the Lord or the man's need, he went hungry.

As I continued down that same sidewalk, I ran across a man with a troubled expression on his face.

"What's wrong?" I asked.

"Somebody just told me about Christ's soon return, His wrath against sin, and His love for sinners. He said if I trust Christ for my salvation, I will be saved and become a child of God, saved from eternal hell. But how do I trust Christ as Savior?"

"You look really burdened," I told him. "What you need to do is relax and think positive. Hey, you haven't killed anybody, right? You look like an outstanding citizen. I'm sure you're a great provider for your family, a good example to society, and I bet you even treat your pets well, don't you?"

"Why, yes I do."

"All you need to know is people appreciate you and love you for your honest character. Your future is going to be bright, I can tell. Just keep doing your best and thinking positive thoughts."

Again, I met the need with a wrong commodity. This man had a spiritual need. He needed to know how to receive Christ as Savior, but instead I gave him an emotional commodity of encouragement to make him feel better about himself. He walked away with his spiritual need still unmet.

Unmet needs cause pain in some dimension of your life. And pain pursues pleasure 100% of the time. People are going to spend time where their needs are met.

Since I didn't give the homeless individual any food, when I walked back down that sidewalk later that night, I found him digging through a garbage can. It's not because he wants to eat trash; it's because he's trying to get his physical need of hunger satiated. It may seem disgusting to think about consuming what he'll pull out of there, but it will meet his immediate need. The same is true with other kinds of needs. You may see a beautiful woman with a guy who treats her like dirt and wonder "why?" Her need for attention wasn't being met, so she turned to this guy. Her basic need for attention was met, even if what she got was trash. There's a balance in life. If you get too little of something, there's pain. If you get too much of something, there's pain. Eating trash is better than not eating at all. Bad love is better than no love.

Ways of Meeting Needs

Harvesting Needs

So we know that people have real needs, and these needs are the driving force behind what they do and the decisions that they make. How you deal with your needs is determined by your character. Who are you really? Do you portray yourself to be something that you're not? The real me is who I am among my family. A person with integrity is a person who is trustworthy even when no one is looking.

When it comes to having your needs met, it's hard to force somebody into a relationship that will meet your needs in a healthy way. So how does it happen? Interestingly, the best way to have your relationship needs met is to meet those of someone else. Be the one who gives an encouraging word to someone who's crestfallen. Put an arm around a friend when they're struggling just to let them know they're not alone in their trial. Share a conversation with an elderly person in a nursing home who doesn't get visitors to talk to. You'd be surprised how fulfilling it is to give of yourself to help somebody in a positive way. Of course, you don't know when and you don't know from whom, but when you meet others needs, it's reciprocated back to you. But remember, if you believe meeting someone else's needs will fulfill your own needs, you're living in a fairy tale. There is no one on this world walking around that is free of needs. Benevolent, generous, kind people have needs just as pressing as yours and mine. The difference? They are preparing themselves for blessings. When we try to harvest the meeting of our needs from a crop that hasn't been planted we'll be sorely disappointed.

There's a universal law at work that is particularly pertinent in relationships. It's called the law of reciprocity which means you reap what you sow. In Galatians 6:7-9, the Bible says, "Don't be misled. Remember that you can't ignore God and get away with it. You will always reap what you sow. Those who live only to satisfy their own sinful desires will harvest the consequences of decay and death. But those who live to please the Spirit will harvest everlasting life from the Spirit. So don't get tired of doing what is good. Don't get discouraged and give up, for we will reap a harvest of blessing at the appropriate time."

There is so much principle about life and eternity in that short scripture. We're going to isolate the relationship aspect out of it.

You reap what you sow. How often have you heard that phrase in your life? Well, what does it mean?

Looking at it from its basic agricultural allusion, what it's saying is what ever seeds you plant in the ground will bring forth not just another seed to take the place of the one you planted, but a harvest that far outnumbers what you've planted. The harvest you receive is determined by what kind of seeds you planted. If you plant apple seeds, you reap apples trees. If you plant thorn or dandelion seeds, you reap a worthless harvest.

In any relationship, if you plant seeds of encouragement, kind words, helpfulness, love, compassion, empathy, or any other positive attitude or action, the Bible promises you will reap a harvest similar to what you've sown but in greater proportion. If you have a need, plant a seed. When you invest your life into others, you will have the initial satisfaction of being able to help somebody else, but you will also cause a ripple effect of consequences that will meet the needs in your life.

Be careful because it works both ways. If you plant despicable seeds of jealousy, envy, slander, hatred, indifference, quick tempers, bad attitudes, and the like, you will also reap the worthless harvest that springs forth from that. When that happens, it's time for you to begin planting for a different harvest.

Keeping the Energy Level

Relationships are complex things that nobody will ever master because every person has their own individual personalities, likes, and dislikes. That's why communication in relationships is key. Remember, communication is more than just having words come out of your mouth. Have you ever heard somebody say to you, "It's not what you said; it's how you said it." Communication is more than just talking. Communication deals with body posture, tone, pitch, and eye contact. In addition to all those, the energy level in communication is a major factor in helping, conversing, and being an encouragement to someone else. Meet someone else's need, and it'll plant seed for your needs to be met one day. The energy of your speech reaches the entire person to whom you're talking. To meet a need you don't cancel out the energy level of your friend, spouse, child or whoever you're talking to, you match energy levels.

If someone is mourning the loss of a loved one or a job, you don't come talk to them with a happy, bouncy tone, saying, "I'm so sorry you lost your job. I'm so sorry you lost your child. I hope everything works out for you." No, the Bible says that we are to mourn with those who mourn. The one who's mourning has a low energy level, and you are to meet them with the same low level of energy so they know you are right there where they're at. In contrast, if someone is rejoicing over great news or a victory, you don't reply with a dead pan expression and a monotone voice saying, "Yeah, I'm so happy for you." The Bible says to rejoice with those who rejoice.

Love has a tone to it. When you speak you can hear love. If you communicate in frustration, anger, or indifference, it is noticeable as well. When you choose a tone in conversation, choose the tone of love.

Making the Connection

Humans were created in pleasure, but sin brought about the experience of pain. Thus, we still tend toward pursuing pleasure even if pleasure is sought in unhealthy ways.

When we experience close, loving and pleasurable relationships—a greater sense of "Us-ness,"—we will find ourselves feeling closely connected, and peaceful.

What does it take to connect in relationships? In a nutshell, it takes intimacy. In today's culture, we associate intimacy with sex, but that's not what I'm talking about here. The Webster's New World Dictionary describes intimacy as being most private and personal, close and familiar, and deep and thorough.

There are two ingredients for intimacy. First, you must be vulnerable, which means you are emotionally open to each other. Second is physical closeness. In married relationships, this may mean holding hands, giving hugs, non-sexual comforting holds. In other relationships, this could entail being in the same room while communicating, maintaining eye contact, respecting the other person as they talk by not gesturing or mocking their words, hand shakes, friendly claps on the shoulder, or a high-five.

We are more open, sharing, vulnerable, and our trust level increases when we are connected in a relationship. However, when you walk in relationship pain—disconnection—you find yourself more guarded, wary, distrustful, and you become more prone to sickness, depression, and maybe even addictions in order to medicate the pain and provide a sense of pleasure for a moment.

Just like exercise is necessary to maintain physical health. Intimacy is paramount to enjoy relationship health.

What Makes Me Better?

Many times in relationships we tend to see the flaws of other people and are provoked to blame them for any problems. When we feel pain, we tend to assign blame. When we experience pleasure we take responsibility for our actions. That's the natural reactions of people in relationships. But we're going to look beyond the circumstantial reactions to what's going on in relationships. We're going to look past what other people do, and take responsibility for both actions and attitudes. It's easy to blame someone else for your faults. "You made me act that way," you might have heard someone say. No one can make you do anything without your permission. When you become responsible for you, you take control of how well the relationship is going to prosper, from the sight of man and from God.

What are some principles I can use to make me more responsible? The Bible, in Matthew 7:12, gives us what is universally known as the "golden rule." *Do for others what you would like them to do for you. This is the summary of all that is taught in the law and the prophets.* Part of being responsible is treating others with dignity and respect. If you don't like the fashion in which some people act toward you, then why do you do the same to other individuals? It is more joyful to your own soul when you are nice to other people—and yes, that includes strangers. When you treat people as you want to be treated, they're more prone to treat you as you wish to be treated.

Take responsibility for your attitude about yourself also. Do you see yourself as being more important than others, or do you choose to make yourself a servant to others?

Jesus said, "Whoever wants to be a leader among you must be your servant, and whoever wants to be first must be slave of all" (Mark 10:44).

According to the Lord, anyone who wants the honor of being a leader or who wants to be prominent should do it by being a servant to others. What does this mean in a relationship? Do you wait hand and foot on everybody, have no agenda of your own, and take meal orders? Of course not. What it does mean is to come to the aid of people who need it. When people are hurting and have spiritual, intellectual, emotional, or physical needs, be the one to help, not the one who looks down on them. If your needs are met, consider yourself blessed, and be willing to shore up others, because there may come a day when you are struggling with a need. The Lord will make sure that the seed you've planted will be the harvest you receive.

How Do You Portray Yourself?

The Bible says, "But those who exalt themselves will be humbled, and those who humble themselves will be exalted" (Matthew 23:12). The Lord hates pride and arrogance. Guess what? People do as well. Have a conversation with a person who thinks he or she is the greatest gift to mankind, and I doubt you'll talk to them a second time.

People who exalt themselves want others to place their attention on them. They want to be admired, praised, and catered to. That builds no trust or connectedness in relationships. Instead, it repels people. Average, everyday people liked to be talked with, not talked down to. Being in the presence of prideful, arrogant people make you feel lesser or just plain disgusted. It's hard to genuinely admire someone who is full of themselves.

When you meet a humble person, you feel comfortable around them. To be humble means you're modest, unpretentious, and conscious of your shortcomings. It doesn't mean you walk around like you think you deserve nothing and that you're the scum of the earth; it just means you know your limitations and you don't have to put on a front for anyone. What people see is what they get. Why do humble people seem so enjoyable to be around? They reflect that they're just regular human beings like all of us who aren't perfect, but instead understanding.

Proud people criticize. Humble people empathize. Arrogant people show no concern for you because they hold deep insecurity and desire to hold up an image. Humble people don't hide behind a mask, and thus can stand beside you to help in whatever you're going through.

The real question is whether you'd choose to be humble or proud. God's kingdom works in reverse of the world. So when you humble yourself, you will be exalted because people will appreciate you for what you've done. If you exalt yourself, your inflated ego can only stay airborne for a while until you discover that others don't think as highly of you as you do.

Listen to this promise from God in 1 Peter 5:6-7. "Humble yourselves under the mighty hand of God, and in good time He will honor you. Give all your worries and cares to God, for He cares about what happens to you."

Judgment vs. Forgiveness

Life is complicated and people aren't perfect. As you live out your life, you will run across people who will disappoint you, hurt you, or abandon you. An observer looking from the outside into a relationship where this happens wouldn't think what you perceive to be emotionally painful to be much at all. But to you in the midst of emotional hurt, it is all too real. There's a choice to be made when this happens. You could either write that person off, inflict revenge or choose to forgive.

There is such power and energy in forgiveness that it brings healing to you and the one who offended you. It cleans the slate, gives a fresh start, and provides a new hope. If you were to mess up, your desire would be for people to have mercy on you. Why be so quick to crush someone else for what they've done?

To condemn or judge someone for what they've done wrong or how they've hurt you has power to it as well. It has the power to belittle someone for a time, but after a while the condemned person will become calloused. The only power you'll have from that point is merely to continue making yourself miserable.

Forgiveness shows maturity. Forgiveness means you're secure enough in yourself to release someone from the consequences of their mistake. To forgive doesn't mean you should overlook habitual sin in someone's life. That takes some prayerful confrontation. When you forgive you show that person that you care about them. Don't expect perfection from people. Expect maturity.

What does God Expect?

What we're going to learn from the past is absolutely contemporary for your life today. In the Old Testament, the nation of Israel had forsaken the Lord who had blessed them immensely. The Lord was calling them back into a right relationship with Him. The Lord desires our relationships to be right with people on earth and with Him. The Lord warned Israel of coming judgment if they didn't repent of their evil ways and trust Him again. In sarcastic response, the rebellious people, in essence, asked, "What should we do to make up for what we've done? Would sacrificing everything make you happy, God? How about if we sacrifice our first-born children, will you be glad then?"

Instead of extinguishing them on the spot, the Almighty Lord answered with compassion and told them what He desired of them, and it all has to do with having right relationships. Having all the riches one could own and having no relationships makes a person truly poor. Remember the island Billy Graham visited and the two people he encountered: the rich businessman and the poor pastor. One was money-rich and relationship-poor, while the other lived on modest means, but enjoyed the love and appreciation of his family and congregation. Who was truly the poor person there?

Recorded in Micah 6:8, the Lord said, "O people, the Lord has already told you what is good, and this is what He requires: to do what is right, to love mercy, and to walk humbly before your God."

He wants us to do the right thing for others. He wants us to be ready to forgive when they wrong us. He wants us to walk humbly before Him which means we understand we aren't the captains of our own destiny or the rule makers. We acknowledge God as supreme, our Creator, and the One who will bless us or discipline us, depending on our obedience to Him.

In Conclusion

What would life be like without relationships? How enjoyable would it be to live in bitterness, disconnection, loneliness, and anger?

Sadly, why do so many teenagers attempt suicide? It's not because they feel there's no reason to live. It's because they think nobody cares about them. When you feel nobody cares, you don't have the drive to live. Even those who wouldn't kill themselves end up dying emotionally if they give up on pursuing healthy relationships.

What would life be like if you had close friendships, loving parents, and a connected spouse? Life would be exciting and wonderful to live. Here's the problem: no relationship is what you'd hope it to be without hard work, sacrifice, and forgiveness.

Life is an adventure.

Human relationships are rewards along the way.

Salvation through Christ is the only way to have a right relationship with God.

Our final destination—Heaven—is a place where relationships with God and people are perfect forever.

Also available from Johnny Earl Jones
You're Gonna Make It:
Extreme Encouragement during Discouraging Times

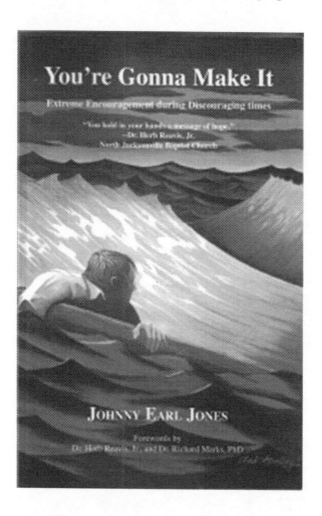

You're Gonna Make It has 25 encouragement-packed chapters with titles such as **Defeating Depression, Forgetting Failure, Refusing Rejection, Handling Heartache,** and more. Notables quoted in the book include **Dr. Charles Stanley, Joel Osteen, Dr. Mike Murdock, Dr. Tony Evans,** and others.

Also available from Johnny Earl Jones
Lifespring
The first-ever Christian adventure romance saga

Check out our website at <u>www.Poisepublishing.com</u> for short synopses or to order **Lifespring** or **You're Gonna Make It.** To arrange Encouragement speaking engagements please contact Johnny Earl Jones at 904-338-3378.